Aspects of England

A Collector's Perspective

Item 32

England's royal arms during Tudor times
from [Bacon's] *Declaration of the . . . Treasons attempted and
committed by . . . [the] Earle of Essex* (1601)

Aspects of England

A Collector's Perspective

An Exhibition at The Grolier Club
March 29 to May 26, 2000

from the collection of

ARTHUR L. SCHWARZ

THE GROLIER CLUB
NEW YORK
2000

This catalogue records an exhibition on view at The Grolier Club
from March 29 to May 26, 2000.

Photography credits: Marlborough Rare Books Ltd: Item 18; Lisa
Martin: Items 4, 5, 8, 14, 16, 21, 23, 30, 32, 54, 56, 60, 68, 71, 77, 82;
Bernard Quaritch Ltd: Item 9.

Printed by The Ascensius Press in an edition of 500 copies.
ISBN 0–910672–31–8
©2000 by ARTHUR L. SCHWARZ

THE GROLIER CLUB
47 East 60th Street
New York, NY
10022

CONTENTS

INTRODUCTION

A BOOK COLLECTION is highly individual and personal. Each collector acquires, within his means, items that he finds particularly interesting and appealing. Some collectors are catholic in their tastes, assembling all kinds of interesting objects with little cohesiveness to the collection as a whole. Others focus on a very narrow area, trying to acquire all the missing pieces, much as a stamp collector tries to fill all the spaces in an album.

This collection certainly falls between these two extremes; indeed, it has been criticized for both being too narrow and also for lacking sufficient focus! No pretense to completeness is made; there are gaping holes in the collection if, for example, one wanted to put together all the important color-plate books about London, or a library specializing in the English Reformation. What the collection does is to provide a serious, but amateur, historian and Anglophile, who also has a love of interesting, old, beautiful books as physical objects, with an outlet which combines all of these interests.

The exhibition is divided into seven sections, each of which has its own theme. Many of the books could have been fitted into categories other than those to which they were assigned. Indeed, among the frustrations in curating this exhibition has been an inability to share additional portions of the selected objects with visitors, and also the necessity of omitting many special items.

The items included in this exhibition have appealed to this collector for their subjects and also as artifacts, in and of themselves, but generally for both qualities. Most of the books are opened to interesting illustrations or to passages relevant to the theme of the section into which each has been placed; others, in one case due to fragility, are open only to their title pages. Some, whose binding is, in itself, important, are displayed unopened. And some of the objects included are not books at all, but panoramas, peep-shows, or documents, the last generally with important seals, and, in one case, just a seal without a document.

Spelling and punctuation in many of these books are strange, by modern standards. Words are even spelled in different ways in the same sentence! I have endeavored to be faithful to the original texts in bibliographical descriptions and quotations, but errors may have crept in. On the other hand, many apparent errors are not such, but I have not used "*sic*" in the literally hundreds of places where I might have.

One last word: this catalogue includes introductory commentary for each section of the exhibition, and for a number of subsections as well. These are not meant to bc definitive discussions in any way but, rather, to place the exhibited items in their proper contexts. With that in mind, I hope that these remarks, as well as the chart of England's royal line of succession, on pages 82 and 83, will help visitors to this exhibition to share in my enthusiasm for England and its history.

ARTHUR L. SCHWARZ

Scarsdale, New York

ACKNOWLEDGMENTS

FIRST and foremost of my acknowledgments and thank-yous I must go to my father, the late Erwin Schwarz, from whom I inherited that strange and wonderful disease, bibliomania. He was the one who started me on the path of book collecting and encouraged me to acquire many of the articles in this exhibition; indeed, some of them were once his. My wife, Susan Teltser-Schwarz, also deserves thanks for putting up with my obsessiveness and for the innumerable hours she has been forced to spend in antiquarian bookshops while I studied many items—some, but not all, of which she actually found exciting.

Many in the book trade have been most helpful, both to my father and to me; Nicholas Poole-Wilson and his colleagues, Richard Linenthal and Ted Hofmann, of Bernard Quaritch Ltd, London, as well as their former associate, Arthur Freeman, have provided valuable guidance for many years. Others whose counsel has helped shape this collection include Jonathan Gestetner and Ian Marr, of Marlborough Rare Books Ltd, London, as well as Chris Coover and Steve Weissman. In mounting this exhibition and writing this catalogue, much assistance was rendered by members and staff of the Grolier Club; especially important have been Eric Holzenberg, Mary Schlosser, Carol Rothkopf, Nancy Houghton, and Michael North.

My thanks to all of you. You have often led me in the right direction; any strayings from the proper path in this exhibition and catalogue are my sole responsibility.

THE EXHIBITION

I
Images of Royalty on Paper, Wax, and Leather
Items 1–17

II
Pomp and Circumstance
Items 18–27

III
Succession and Its Stumbling Blocks
Items 28–41

IV
Social Commentary
Items 42–45

V
Royal, Civil, and Ecclesiastical Architecture
Items 46–64

VI
The English Reformation
Items 65–80

VII
Humor
Items 81–84

I

Images of Royalty on Paper, Wax, and Leather

W<small>E</small>, today, are more familiar with the likenesses of many English monarchs than were their contemporaries. Before modern communications and published portraits, kings and queens had the problem of recognizability; a king was known by his attire, his crown, and the other symbols of his power. A monarch's seal proclaimed his splendor and titles for all to see, although some laid claim to titles that might not really be theirs. This portion of the exhibition deals with these royal images and their projection; some are contemporary with the subject, while others are later.

1.   Henry Noel Humphreys. *A Record of the Black Prince*. London: Longman, *et al.*, 1849.

A highly successful Victorian gift or table book, this item is shown closed to display the publisher's binding of black plaster over *papier mâché*, with its royal motif. Each cover is a pierced and molded black relief plaque including the English royal arms on a shield. Note the French *fleurs de lys*, included at a time when English kings also styled themselves as kings of France. Although recent research has questioned whether or not these bindings are, in fact, molded and stained *papier mâché*, no satisfactory alternative has been offered.

2.   Henry Shaw. *Dresses and Decorations of the Middle Ages from the seventh century to the seventeenth century*. London: William Pickering, 1843. Two volumes.

Ruari McLean, in *Victorian Book Design*, said that this book "has a considerable claim to be called the most handsome book produced in the whole of the nineteenth century; some of Ackermann's volumes of aquatints [many of which are included in this exhibition] . . . may run it close, but they are much less handsome typographically." In addition to the detailed copper-plate engravings, the text is "adorned with elaborate initials and decorations printed in colour from wood-blocks. . . ."[1]

1. Ruari McLean, *Victorian Book Design and Colour Printing* (London: 1972) p. 66.

Opened to the portrait of Richard II, king of England from 1377 to 1399. Son of Edward the Black Prince (died 1376) and grandson of King Edward III, Richard succeeded to his grandfather's throne in June 1377. As he was not yet of age, his government was dominated by his uncle, John of Gaunt, duke of Lancaster. Richard's reign was filled with difficulties, including economic deterioration caused by the Black Death of the mid-fourteenth century, intermittent war with France, and the Peasants' Revolt of 1381. There were continuing conflicts with the nobility and, following John of Gaunt's death, Richard attempted to confiscate the vast Lancastrian estates; John's son, Henry Bolingbroke, who was in a ten-year forced exile for "treason," invaded England and Richard surrendered without a fight. He abdicated in favor of Bolingbroke, who ascended the throne as King Henry IV. Richard was imprisoned in Pontefract Castle, where he died four months later, possibly by starving himself to death.

3. **Francis [Bacon].** *The Historie of the Raigne of King Henry The Seuenth.* **London: Printed by W. Stansby for Matthew Lownes, and William Barret, 1622.**

The first edition of the classic biography of Henry VII, the first Tudor monarch. "Every history that has been written since has derived all its light from this, and followed its guidance in every question of importance."[2] Note the caption on the king's portrait: "The Heart of an Inscrutable King," and the symbols of his power: crowns, the Order of the Garter, the orb and scepter, as well as the Tudor rose.

4. *Imitations of Original Drawings by Hans Holbein, in the Collection of His Majesty, . . . for the Portraits of Illustrious Persons of the Court of Henry VIII.* **London: Printed by W. Bulmer & Co., Shakspeare Printing Office, 1792–1800.**

Hans Holbein the Younger produced many drawings of the members of Henry VIII's court: officials, soldiers, politicians, humanists, family members, and friends. The ownership history of the drawings is complex; among other things, Queen Caroline of Ansbach, wife of King George II, "found" them in a bureau in Kensington Palace and had them framed as wall hangings. Early in the reign of George III,

2. *Dictionary of National Biography* (New York: 1885) Vol. II, p. 351.

Item 4

Holbein's portrait of Queen Jane Seymour (1795)

the drawings were removed from their frames, stuck onto the pages of two volumes, and placed in the king's library at Buckingham House. Here they were copied by Francesco Bartolozzi in a series of eighty-four stipple engravings and published by the Royal Librarian.

Abbey commented that this is "in every way a splendid book, the colour printing reproducing with extraordinary fidelity the original designs."[3] And Gordon Ray said that "this magnificent work is surely the finest early example of English color printing."[4] Rare in parts, this copy was formerly in the possession of the Romanoff family; much of the text is accompanied by handwritten translations into French.

The portraits exhibited here are of Jane Seymour, third wife of Henry VIII, and of their son, Edward, who would inherit his father's throne in 1547. Jane was a lady-in-waiting to Henry's second wife, Anne Boleyn, when the king became infatuated with her, assuredly a key factor in Anne's downfall and beheading. Unfortunately, Henry and Jane's marriage lasted less than eighteen months, as Jane died only twelve days after giving birth to Henry's only legitimate male heir. For the rest of his life Henry grieved for her, perhaps because he saw her as the only one of his wives who hadn't "done him wrong," excepting Catherine Parr, who married him when he was old and infirm and who survived him.

Edward VI died of tuberculosis in 1553 at the age of fifteen, not having achieved his majority; he never truly ruled his kingdom nor put a personal stamp on his reign. During his regime, however, Protestantism gained a firm foothold in England, due to his support and to that of his protectors; at Edward's death, however, his Roman Catholic half-sister, Mary, became queen and instituted a Catholic counter-reformation which was ended only by her death after but five years on the throne. *(See illustration, page 9.)*

* * * *

SEALS are devices used to authenticate documents, to indicate the authority under which they were written, and to testify, as well, to the person taking responsibility for the contents. The earliest English seals were "pendant"; that is, they were hung by cords or thin strips of parchment

3. *Life in England in Aquatint and Lithography: 1770–1860 . . . From the Library of J. R. Abbey* (London: 1953) p. 144.

4. Gordon N. Ray, *The Illustrator and the Book in England from 1790 to 1914* (New York: 1976) p. 20.

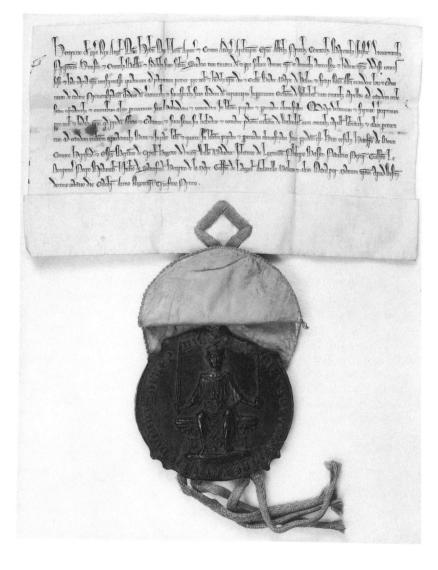

Item 5
Document with seal of King Henry III (1247)

from the documents themselves, similar to papal bulls (from the Latin "*bulla*," "seal"),[5] but they were made of wax, unlike the leaden bulls.

Pendant seals were permanent and survived the first reading of a document. Only later were seals used to close documents; while this had the advantage of indicating that the contents had not been tampered with, the seals themselves were destroyed when the documents were opened and could not, therefore, be used as a means of permanent authentication. *(See Item 14, letters of George I.)* Pendant seals are still in use, however, for particularly important documents *(Item 41)* and even for many of seemingly less interest except, of course, to their recipients *(Item 15)*.

Saying that pendant seals were "permanent" is a bit of an exaggeration; however, considering their age—Item 5 is over 750 years old—and the fragility of the beeswax from which they were fashioned, these seals are in remarkable condition. In most of the items exhibited here, the documents are of distinctly less interest than their seals and, therefore, several parchment documents which have been stored folded for many years are shown that way.

5. Henry III, king of England. *Document with royal seal, letters patent granting the Church of Walsall, Staffordshire, to Abbott Richard and the Convent of Halesowen.* Westminster: 18 October 1247.

> Pendant to the document is the first great seal of Henry III, cast from a pair of matrices designed in 1218. The images have been created in deep relief depicting, on the obverse, Henry enthroned in majesty and, on the reverse, the mounted king in battle attire.[6] His titles, in the surrounding texts, are king of England and lord of Ireland (obv.), and duke of Normandie and Aquitaine and count of Anjou (rev.). A second great seal was created for Henry in 1259, omitting the titles of duke of Normandie and count of Anjou which he had lost that year as a result of the Treaty of Paris.
>
> The great seal, itself, has been preserved in its original protective bag of pink doeskin. *(See illustration, page 11.)*

---

5. The word "bull" can mean the leaden seal attached to the pope's edict or, alternatively, the edict, itself.

6. From the time of William II until the present day, almost all great seals have depicted, on the front, the enthroned monarch and, on the back, the monarch mounted on a horse.

6. **Edward III, king of England.** *Document with royal seal, letters patent granting license to enfeoffe of Walter de Peveseye of the Manor of Wolveton in the Isle of Wight.* Woodstock: 26 June 1332.

Exhibited here is the second of Edward III's seven great seals; its images are conceptually similar to those on the seal of Henry III *(Item 5)*. Here, however, the king's pose is "with knees pushed to one side and a subtle bend in the waist. Such stylishness was part of the currency of European royal seals at the period . . . , probably under French influence."[7] The inscriptions, most of which are lacking in this example, still proclaim the English monarch as king of England, lord of Ireland and duke of Aquitaine. From 1337 onward, Edward styled himself, in addition, as king of France and his sixth seal (1340) reflected this claim. His seventh seal, created after the Treaty of Brétigny in 1360, omitted this title, but its text was reworked in 1371 to include the claim once again.

7. **Edward IV, king of England.** *Document with royal seal, letters patent to the Manor of Melton Constable.* Westminster: 30 October 1483.

Not only does the text surrounding the enthroned king include claim to the throne of France, the king's scepter is now topped by a *fleur de lys*, France's traditional symbol.

8. **Henry VIII, king of England.** *Document with royal seal, letters patent granting to William Wybarn of Begham, Sussex, and his son John the manors of Pepynbury, Kent [formerly owned by Thomas Cromwell], and Tyllingdowe, Surrey, and other properties in St. Sepulchre, London, and elsewhere.* Westminster: 8 May 1545.

Note, on this document, the initial letter portrait of Henry VIII, in pen and ink within the initial "H," the engrossed historiated majuscules in the first line, and the upper margin decorated with heraldic beasts and emblems. The seal is the third used by Henry VIII and is in the Renaissance style, using roman, not black-letter forms. Henry

7. Jonathan Alexander and Paul Binski, eds., *Age of Chivalry: Art in Plantagenet England 1200–1400* (London: 1987) p. 494.

Item 8

Document with seal of King Henry VIII (1545)
(Detail: Initial letter portrait of Henry VIII)

is proclaimed not only as king and as Defender of the Faith, but as Supreme Head on Earth of the Church of England, the title he adopted after the 1534 Act of Supremacy; this last title was renounced by the Roman Catholic Queen Mary in 1553 but readopted—in altered form, as "Supreme Governor"—by Queen Elizabeth in 1559. *(See illustration, facing page.)*

9. **Elizabeth I, queen of England.** *Royal seal, designed and engraved by Nicholas Hilliard, detached from a document.* (ca. 1584–1603).

Writing of England's Virgin Queen, Winston Churchill said that "she had a capacity for inspiring devotion that is perhaps unparalleled among British sovereigns. There may be something grotesque to modern eyes in the flattery paid her by the Court, but with her people she never went wrong. By instinct she knew how to earn popular acclaim. In a sense her relationship with her subjects was one long flirtation. She gave to her country the love that she never entirely reposed in any one man, and her people responded with a loyalty that almost amounted to worship. It is not for nothing that she has come down to history as Good Queen Bess."[8]

The designer of this seal was Nicholas Hilliard, the first great native-born English painter of the Renaissance, known primarily for the art of painting miniature portraits. Hilliard's earliest known attempts at miniature painting were in 1560; he became miniaturist to Queen Elizabeth I about 1570, created many portraits of the queen and of leading courtiers, and, in 1584, designed the queen's second great seal. *(See illustration, page 16.)*

10. **James I, king of England.** *Document with royal seal, letters patent creating Thomas Littleton a baronet.* **Westminster: 25 July 1618.**

Over the years, the great seal became larger and still more ornate. The diameter of James's seal is 15 cm., compared with the 10 cm. diameter of Henry III's, Item 5 in this exhibition, designed almost 400 years earlier. The text on each face declares James to be king of England, Scotland, France, and Ireland and the obverse includes renderings of the shield of the Order of the Garter on each side of the enthroned king.

8. Winston S. Churchill, *The New World* (Volume II of *A History of the English-Speaking Peoples*) (New York: 1966) p. 103.

Item 9
Hilliard's seal for Queen Elizabeth I (ca. 1584–1603)

11. **Charles I, king of England.** *Document with royal seal, letters patent.* **Westminster: 17 July 1631.**

Charles I's seal proclaims him as king of Scotland, England, France, and Ireland—in that order—as well as Defender of the Faith, the title originally granted to Henry VIII. Here, more than seventy-five years after England had lost Calais, the last remnant of its medieval empire on the continent of Europe, English kings continued to style themselves as kings of France; the English royal coat of arms included the French *fleurs de lys* until the middle of the eighteenth century, in the reign of George III. Also clearly discernible are the harp (for Ireland) and two styles of lions, representing courage and strength (for Scotland and England).

12. **Oliver Cromwell, lord protector of England.** *Document with the great seal of the Commonwealth, letters patent by Oliver Cromwell appointing Sir Henry Lyttleton as sheriff of the County of Worcester.* **Westminster: 15 November 1654.**

This document's seal is, of course, not "royal," being that of the Puritan Commonwealth under Oliver Cromwell. On the seal's obverse, parliament has replaced the enthroned monarch, since the people, not the king, were the perceived source of power and authority *(see Item 36, Milton's* The Tenure of Kings and Magistrates*)*; it bears the text "1651 In the Third Year of Freedom by God's Blessing Restored." The text on the reverse, "The Great Seal of England," surrounds a map of England and Ireland. Scotland, which had proclaimed Charles I's son as King Charles II following his father's execution, did not recognize the Commonwealth and, therefore, is not depicted on this map.

13. **Charles II, king of England.** *Document signed, countersigned "Arlington" [Henry Bennet, earl of Arlington], ordering the payment of salaries for the councillors of the Foreign Plantations, including the earl of Sandwich as president of the Council.* **Whitehall: 2 November 1670.**

Arlington, following the execution of Charles I, allied himself with the royal family in exile, and became secretary of state and especial confidant of Charles II. He seems to have been as unscrupulous as he could safely be while in the Cabal[9] ministry where he directed foreign affairs, of which he was in charge, to his personal advantage. He became connected to the royal family through the marriage of his daughter Isabella to Henry Fitzroy, duke of Grafton, the illegitimate but officially recognized son of Charles II and Barbara Villiers, duchess of Cleveland.

The document, itself, is undistinguished; it is manually signed "Charles R" at its head, unlike more personal correspondence which requires a reader to look at the conclusion to identify the author. *(See Item 14, letters of George I.)*

14. **George I, king of England.** *Four letters, comprising (1) to King Louis XV, king of France, and (2) to the duchess of Orléans, both letters introducing Horatio Walpole as envoy extraordinary to Paris and signed "George R"; (3) addressed to the duke of Orléans and (4) addressed to the duke of Bourbon, sealed and unopened (but presumably signed). (1) St. James's: 13 January 1724; (2) St. James's: 13 May 1724.*

In January 1724, George I appointed Horatio Walpole (a diplomat, politician, and younger brother of Sir Robert Walpole, the first British Prime Minister) as an envoy extraordinary to the court of France and wrote a number of formal letters of introduction for his new emissary. Walpole initially refused the post, however; when he finally accepted it, in March of that year, the original letters were outdated and they lay among the Walpole family effects for many years. Two of these letters are signed by George I, one at the time of Walpole's initial appointment, and the other while he was in Paris; the signature at the bottom of each letter emphasizes the relationship between sender and recipient. Since the other two have never been opened, one has to trust their provenance and hope they are what they appear to be. *(See illustration, facing page.)*

9. Charles II ruled through a group of five ministers chosen in 1667 and known as the "Cabal," suggesting secrecy and intrigue and also, coincidentally, an anagram of the first letters of their names.

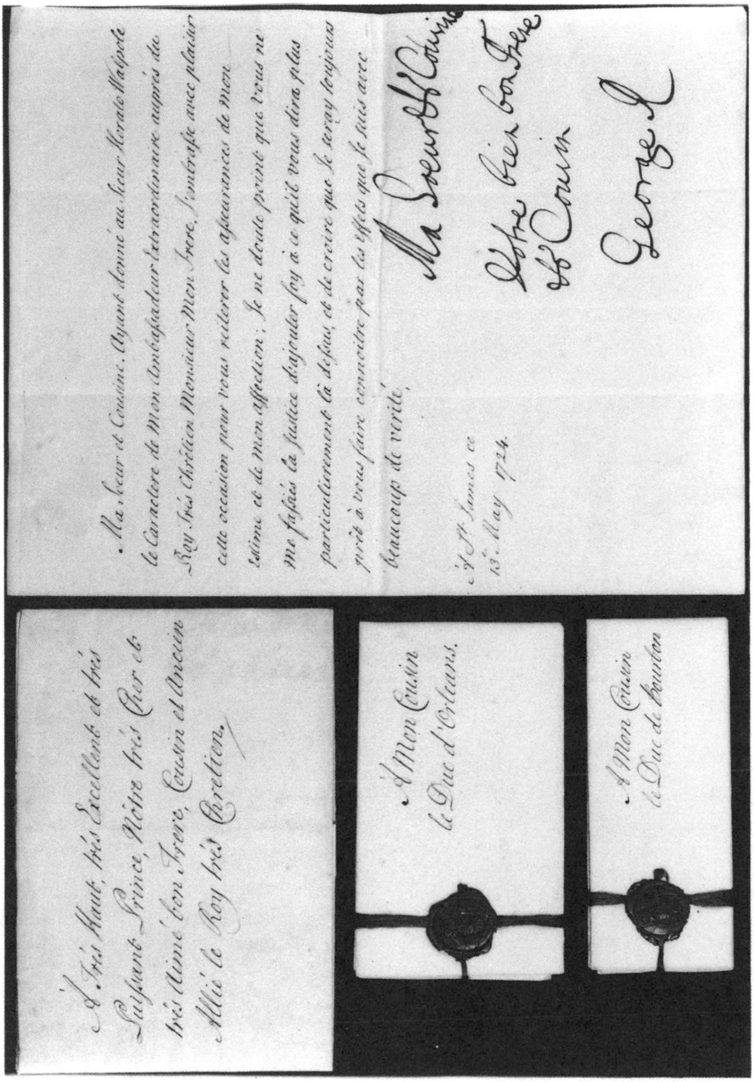

Item 14
Four letters from King George I (two unopened) (1724)

15. **Victoria, queen of England.** *Document with royal seal, letters patent granting to Aimé Rieder a grant of patent rights respecting certain shades, spectacles, and eye glasses.* [Westminster]: **6 May 1864.**

The reverse of the yellow wax seal bears a now simplified claim, "Victoria by the Grace of God Queen of Britain and Defender of the Faith." On the obverse, visible here, the enthroned monarch holds the orb and scepter, symbols of her power, and is flanked by two female attendants.

Rieder, a French inventor, was active in creating new designs for the framing of spectacles, stereoscopic viewers, opera glasses, and the like.

＊ ＊ ＊ ＊

16. *The Form and Order of the Service that is to be Performed and of the Ceremonies that are to be Observed in the Coronation of their Majesties King George V and Queen Mary in the Abbey Church of S. Peter, Westminster on Thursday, the 22nd Day of June, 1911.* London: **Novello and Company, 1911.**

The Prince of Wales's copy of the order of service for the coronation of his parents, one of 150 copies privately printed and bound for presentation. Prince Edward's elaborately bound copy—which was personalized by the addition of the Prince of Wales's feathers—is number 3 of this limited edition; presumably copies 1 and 2 were retained by King George and Queen Mary. The blue morocco covers are elaborately gilt, each with a floral border and large central plaque incorporating the royal coat-of-arms surrounded by crowned initials "G" and "R" and the crowned emblems of England, Scotland and Ireland, all on checkerboard grounds with alternating squares filled with Tudor roses; the smooth spine is gilt lettered with the Prince of Wales's feathers gilt at head and foot; the gilt-ruled turn-ins have the Prince of Wales's feathers gilt in the corners. The original owner of this volume became King Edward VIII and, following his abdication, the duke of Windsor. *(See illustration, facing page.)*

Item 16

The Form and Order of the Service that is to be Performed . . . in the Coronation of
their Majesties King George V and Queen Mary (front cover of the copy
which was specially bound for their son, the Prince of Wales,
later King Edward VIII and duke of Windsor) (1911)

17. *The Music with the Form and Order of the Service to be Performed at the Coronation of Her Most Excellent Majesty Queen Elizabeth II.* **London: Novello and Company, 1953.**

The full (faded) crimson morocco binding with the arms of the queen, surrounded by an elaborate gilt frame, is suitably elegant for the occasion, but clearly less so than the similar volume printed for the coronation of George V, which had been specially bound for his son Edward, Prince of Wales (*Item 16*).

Number 139 of an edition limited to 150 copies.

II

Pomp and Circumstance

Even today, England has retained its ancient attachment to pomp and circumstance, fanfare and hoopla. Although British sovereigns have little real power, the ceremony attached to royal coronations, weddings, and funerals is watched by millions world-wide on television, and hundreds of thousands of visitors come to London each year and crowd outside the Buckingham Palace railings and elsewhere for the Changing of the Guard and other ceremonies. This portion of the exhibition includes printed material celebrating coronations, weddings, military might, and other great events from the seventeenth to the twentieth century.

18. **[Jean Puget] de la Serre.** *Histoire de l'Entree de la Reyne Mere dv Roy Tres-Chrestien, dans la Grande-Bretaigne.* **London: J. Raworth for George Thomason and Octavian Pullen, 1639.**

This lovely volume includes a series of plates which describe the visit of Marie de Médicis, queen-mother of King Louis XIII of France and widow of the assassinated Henry IV, to her daughter and son-in-law, Queen Henrietta Maria and King Charles I of England. Marie, having been banished by her son, the king, for her complicity in a plot against his chief minister, Richelieu, had escaped imprisonment and fled to the Spanish Netherlands in 1631, never to return to France. In 1638, being unwelcome in The Hague, to which she had recently moved from Brussels, Marie sought refuge and asylum with her daughter, the queen of England.

The plates include views of Harwich, where Marie landed (she was prevented from landing at Dover due to storms), and Colchester, the *feu de joie* on the Thames, and four interior and exterior views of St. James's Palace. Most important in terms of this exhibition is the large folding view of Marie's splendid entry into London and the progress of the royal party along Cheapside. In addition to what appears to be an eye-witness's visual account of the event, this charming, if technically unsophisticated, plate is a wonderful record of the architecture and building decoration along a principal London street, more than 360 years ago. *(See illustration, page 24.)*

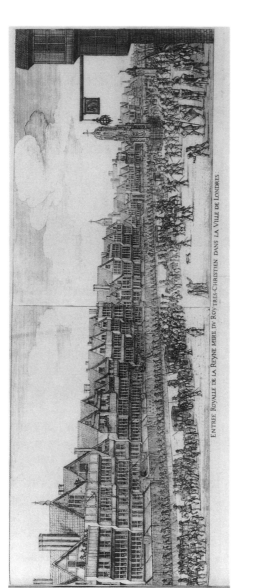

Item 18

Entrance of Marie de Médicis into London from [Puget] de la Serre's *Histoire de l'Entree de la Reyne Mere du Roy Tres-Chrestien, dans la Grande-Bretaigne* (1639)

19. **Francis Sandford.** *The History of the Coronation Of* . . . *James II* . . . *And* . . . *Queen Mary* . . . . **London: Printed by Thomas Newcomb, 1687.**

Called the "most important descriptive book" of the late seventeenth century, Sandford's work fully reflects the "grave and pompous" occasion and "James's exalted notions of his kingly office."[10] It became the record on which all future coronations were based; every minute detail of ritual and dress is meticulously covered. The author, Francis Sandford, was Lancaster herald of arms and official historian of the coronation. Shown here is the plate depicting the splendid dinner which followed the coronation of James II and Queen Mary.

Their reign was to be a very short one; due to his Roman Catholic beliefs, James was driven into exile in the "Glorious Revolution" of 1688. (*See [John] Michael Wright's* An Account of . . . (the) . . . Earl of Castlemaine's Embassy, *Item 39.*)

20. *Engraved ticket of admission to the coronation of George III, king of England.* **[N.P.: n.p.], 1761.**

The "SPQB" carved on the stone capital suggests that the might of Britain in the eighteenth century rivaled that of ancient Rome, with its capitals carved with an "SPQR," standing for "the Senate and people of Rome."

21. **Edward Orme.** *The Battles of The British Army in Portugal, Spain And France, From the Year 1808 to 1814. Under the Command of Englands Great Captain Arthur Duke of Wellington.* **London: Edward Orme, 1815.**

This item comprises thirteen circular colored aquatint views of battles of the British army in the Napoleonic Wars. Hinged together with a medal-shaped bronze container, the views form a connected series with a circular engraved title at each end. Commemorated are Wellington's victories in the Peninsular War, where he and his British troops supported Spain's and Portugal's rebellions against France, as well as his later triumphs in France proper. The panels are

10. Ifan Kyle Fletcher, "The Literature of Splendid Occasions in English History," *The Library,* 5th ser., vol. I, nos. 3, 4 (1946–47) p. 193.

Item 21

Title page and the Battle of Waterloo from Orme's *The Battles of the British Army . . .* (1815)

in chronological order, reading from right to left; the final view depicts the now classic allied victory over Napoleon at Waterloo, for which Britain received most of the credit, a fact which contributed to her leadership in Europe and much of the rest of the world for many years. *(See illustration, facing page.)*

22. [F. W. Blagdon]. *An Historical Memento, Representing the Different Scenes of Public Rejoicing . . . in Celebration of The Glorious Peace of 1814, and of The Centenary of the Accession of the Illustrious House of Brunswick to The Throne of these Kingdoms.* London: Edward Orme, 1814.

The text of this volume is no less jingoistic than its lengthy title, and it gives full vent to British pride in the defeat and abdication of Napoleon, *viz.*:

> It is not necessary to enter into the particulars of the horrid French Revolution; for, had the people of France confined themselves to the new-modelling of their government, according to their ideas of the change being a national benefit, however absurd and irrational they might have been, the wise administration of this country would never have interposed to stop their progress. But when, after destroying their own legitimate government, they, in an official decree of the 19th of November, 1792, declared '*war to palaces,*' and openly avowed their determination to assist any other people who would imitate their example, it became high time for this country to set aside that system of neutrality which it had so sincerely professed and endeavoured to maintain.[11]

The six colored aquatint plates which complement the text have been called "the finest memento of the occasion."[12]

23. Henry Alken and George Augustus Sala. *The Funeral Procession of Arthur Duke of Wellington.* London: R. Ackermann, [1852].

"Panoramas are perhaps used at their best in recording great processions, and the finest English example of this kind is *The Funeral of the Duke of Wellington* by H. Alken and G. A. Sala."[13] This extensive panorama of 28 linen-backed colored aquatints measures over 66

11. Pp. 8–9.
12. Bernard Adams, *London Illustrated: 1604–1851* (London: 1983) p. 258.
13. *Life in England . . . J. R. Abbey,* p. xxi.

feet in length when extended and certainly conveys and preserves the grandeur of this monumental state funeral. *(See illustration, facing page.)*

24. *Lane's Telescopic View. of the Ceremony of Her Majesty Opening the Great Exhibition . . . Designed by [Thomas J.] Rawlins.* **London: C. A. Lane, 1851.**

"Telescopic views," or "peep shows," were popular, if rudimentary, three-dimensional representations of some of the grander scenes. In this one, a viewer, looking through the hole at one end, could see the length of the Crystal Palace, the huge Hyde Park iron and glass exhibition hall that was home to the Great Exhibition of 1851 and which Queen Victoria compared to a "fairyland." There were about 14,000 exhibitors, and the participants, from around the globe, included India, Australia, New Zealand, and other far-flung British outposts, as well as the United States, France, and other non-British entities. Meant to display Britain's worldwide economic and political leadership, the Great Exhibition was a resounding success.

The title of this work may be a bit misleading, as one cannot actually see the queen while looking through the peep-hole; she is standing on the red-carpeted steps but is hidden from view by the fountain.

25. **W. H. Russell.** *The Wedding at Windsor.* **London: Day and Son, [1864].**

This volume provides a detailed description of the wedding of Albert Edward, Prince of Wales and Princess Alexandra Caroline of Denmark (later King Edward VII and Queen Alexandra). The site was St. George's Chapel, Windsor, which had been designed as the Chapel of the Order of the Garter and still contains much of the Order's paraphernalia. Begun in 1475 in the reign of Edward IV and completed in that of Henry VIII in 1528, it is, along with the Henry VII Chapel at Westminster Abbey *(see Items 57, 58, and 59)* and King's College Chapel, Cambridge *(see Item 54)*, among the finest examples of Perpendicular Gothic architecture. It is second only to Westminster Abbey as a site for royal burial and Edward and Alexandra were interred there.

We can get a feeling for the splendor of this occasion from Robert Dudley's plate of "The Marriage" with the elegant attire of participants and guests, the Beefeaters on guard, and the groom's mother, Queen Victoria, watching the proceedings from the Royal Closet *(top center).*

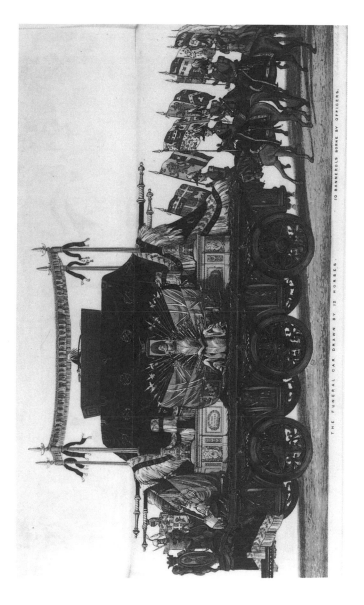

Item 23

Alken and Sala's *Funeral Procession of Arthur Duke of Wellington* (detail) (1852)

26. Winston S. Churchill. *A Speech by The Prime Minister the Right Honourable Winston Churchill in the House of Commons. August 20th, 1940.* [London]: The Baynard Press, 1940.

In the summer of 1940, Churchill spoke of his nation's debt to the fighter pilots of the Royal Air Force who were all that stood between Britain and complete destruction from the air. His words were a rallying point for his countrymen at a very bleak time in their nation's history:

> The gratitude of every home in our Island, in our Empire, and indeed throughout the world, except in the abodes of the guilty, goes out to the British airmen who, undaunted by odds, unwearied in their constant challenge and mortal danger, are turning the tide of world war by their prowess and by their devotion. *Never in the field of human conflict was so much owed by so many to so few.* (Emphasis added.)[14]

This first separate edition of Churchill's speech was published simultaneously with the *Parliamentary Debates*, the British equivalent of the American *Congressional Record*.

27. *The Royal Wedding: The Marriage of H.R.H. The Prince of Wales and The Lady Diana Spencer: St. Paul's Cathedral 29 July 1981.* [London]: Royal Jubilee Trusts, 1981.

The official program for the marriage of Charles, Prince of Wales, and Lady Diana Spencer, published for the general public at a price of 50 pence. It is illustrated with portraits of Charles and Diana, the archbishop of Canterbury and the dean of St. Paul's, the state coaches used in the procession, and a map of the processional route from Buckingham Palace to St. Paul's and return. The paper wrapper bears the arms of the Prince of Wales on the top cover.

14. P. 10.

III

Succession and Its Stumbling Blocks

A MAJOR objective of any monarch has always been to assure the line of succession and to provide a blood line to inherit the power and the throne, itself. This has often proved to be problematical, and in many eras of English history succession has been a critical issue for a monarch and the people; indeed, tension, conflict, and bloodshed have too often been the result of the lack of an obvious, acceptable heir to the crown. The following discussion, greatly simplified but complex nevertheless, is intended to enable a visitor to this exhibition to place the displayed items in their historical context.

Most of this section of the exhibition concerns Tudor and Stuart England, the periods which started with the accession of Henry VII in 1485 and ended in 1714 with the death of Queen Anne. Two other items, from the Windsor monarchy, are of a much later period.

In August 1485, Henry Tudor, a distant Lancastrian claimant to the throne, defeated the unpopular Yorkist, Richard III, at Bosworth Field, effectively ending the Wars of the Roses. To unite the two warring families, Henry, now Henry VII of England, married Elizabeth of York, Richard's niece (and sister of the two princes whom Richard is thought to have murdered while they were held captive in the Tower of London). King Henry had two sons who survived childhood, Prince Arthur and Prince Henry. Arthur married Catherine of Aragon, daughter of Ferdinand and Isabella of Spain, but he died shortly after his marriage, and orderly succession then depended on the continued good health of Prince Henry. King Henry's wife also died and the king briefly considered marriage to Catherine to secure her dowry and inheritances, but he thought better of it and he then contemplated a marriage with the young dowager queen of Naples. Item 28 is the first printing, some 250 years after the event, of the questions asked by King Henry VII of his ambassadors who had been sent to meet and then report back on this possible new bride.

One of the most famous succession issues of English history involves Henry VII's second son, who inherited the throne as Henry VIII on his father's death in 1509. Henry VIII married his brother's widow, Catherine of Aragon, after receiving a papal bull from Julius II dispensing with the bar of affinity created by Catherine's marriage to Prince Arthur. After over fifteen years of marriage, Henry & Catherine's only surviving child was a daughter, Mary; Henry, concerned about his lack of a male heir, began to wonder whether in granting the dispensation the pope had exceeded his papal powers and that Henry and Catherine had, indeed, contravened the law of God.[15] The combination of Henry's real or imagined scruples, his infatuation with Anne Boleyn, and clear dynastic urgency led him to seek a divorce from Catherine but political alliances made this extremely difficult. When Henry sought to have the dispensation voided he was opposed by Holy Roman Emperor Charles V, who was holding Pope Clement VII in virtual imprisonment and also just happened to be Catherine's nephew! Item 29, Tyndale's *The practyse of Prelates*, deals at length with the question of whether the king should be permitted to divorce his wife on the grounds that she had been his brother's wife. The issue of the divorce, "the king's great matter," eventually led to Cardinal Wolsey's downfall for his inability to persuade the pope, to the breach with Rome, and to the establishment of the Church of England as a separate Church with Henry and his successors at its head.

Henry married a total of six times but only one male heir survived him. Edward, the son of Henry's third wife, Jane Seymour, became Edward VI at his father's death, but he lived only to the age of fifteen. Although Edward had two half-sisters, Mary and Elizabeth, both had been declared illegitimate, and therefore ineligible to inherit the throne, as Henry voided one marriage after another. The duke of Northumberland, who served as "protector" at the end of Edward's reign, tried to continue in power by putting his daughter-in-law, Lady Jane Grey, a great-granddaughter of Henry VII, on the throne. Their forces were overcome by those of Mary Tudor who, although a Roman Catholic, was the daughter of Henry VIII by Catherine of Aragon and had great popular support; Jane was forced out after only nine days as queen and she and her supporters received the punishment of traitors: beheading.

Queen Mary also lived only a few years after ascending to the throne and was succeeded by her half-sister, Elizabeth, daughter of Henry VIII and Anne Boleyn. Although not lacking suitors, Elizabeth I never married, and succession was an important issue throughout her reign. One potential claimant was her cousin, Mary, queen of Scots, who might become queen of England as well as Scotland on Elizabeth's death, and if Elizabeth just happened to die young then Mary might inherit just that much the

---

15. Leviticus 18:6–18 recites the various degrees of affinity in which marriages of near relations are unlawful; it goes on (Lev. 20:21) to say that "if a man shall take his brother's wife, it is an unclean thing: . . . they shall be childless." On the other hand, Henry chose to ignore the dictate of Deuteronomy 26:5 in which a man is commanded, should his brother die childless, to "take her [his sister-in-law] to him to wife."(Authorized Version)

sooner. The result was the famous enmity between the two and Mary's execution, by Elizabeth's order, in 1587. Mary, herself, had been no stranger to the use of violence to solve her problems. *(See Item 31).*

When Elizabeth died, unmarried and childless, in 1603, the throne passed to a distant cousin, King James VI of Scotland, son of Mary, queen of Scots; he then ruled as James I of England. He was succeeded by his son, the authoritarian Charles I, whose conservative religious views and, in particular, claims of the divine right of kings, led to his trial, conviction as a traitor, and beheading in 1649. Three items *(Items 34, 35, and 36)* concern the reign and death of Charles I.

During the Commonwealth period, England was ruled without a king but by the lord protector, Oliver Cromwell, although Charles I's son had been crowned as Charles II, in exile. *(Item 37).* The Protectorate fell and the monarchy was restored in 1660, although Charles II always dated his reign from the date of his father's death in 1649. Upon the death of Charles II, his brother came to the throne as James II; James, however, was deposed in the "Glorious Revolution," due largely to his obdurate Roman Catholicism *(Item 39)*, and was succeeded in 1688 by his daughter Mary, and her husband, William of Orange (who was a grandson of Charles I).

The final items in this portion of the exhibition concern Edward VIII's renunciation of the throne, in 1936, in order to marry a divorced commoner, Wallis Simpson, "the woman I love." Exhibited are the official report of his abdication and also the warrant of his brother, who succeeded him as George VI, naming the former king as duke of Windsor, *(Items 40 and 41).*

28. Henry VII, king of England. *Instructions given by King Henry the Seventh, to his embassadors, When he intended to marry The young Queen of Naples: together with the Answers of the Embassadors.* London: Printed for T. Becket, and P. A. De Hondt, 1761.

The young dowager queen of Naples[16] had been suggested as a second wife for Henry VII by Queen Isabella of Castile, who wished to divert him from thoughts of her daughter (and his daughter-in-law), Catherine of Aragon, dowager Princess of Wales, widow of Arthur, Prince of Wales and eventually wife of King Henry VIII.[17] Where his son, Henry VIII, would later send Hans Holbein to paint a portrait of a recommended bride, Anne of Cleves, Henry VII sent ambassadors with a paper detailing the king's questions.

16. Joan, widow of Ferdinand II of Naples, and niece of Ferdinand of Aragon.
17. See Garrett Mattingly, *Catherine of Aragon* (London: 1942) pp. 52ff. for a discussion of Henry VII's consideration of Catherine as a prospective bride.

The king here seeks to know about the clearness of the young woman's skin, the color of her hair, the condition of her teeth, the size and shape of her nose, and a good deal more. Article XVI asks the ambassadors "to marke hir brestes and pappes whether they be bigge or smale." The answer was as follows: "As to thys Articule the said quynes brestes be somewhat grete & fully & in as muche as that they were trussid somewhat highe after the maner of [her] contrey the whiche causithe hir grace for to seme muche the fullyer & hir necke to be the shorter."[18] The next question asked whether she had any hair on her upper lip. In fact the lady apparently passed muster physically, but the marriage never came about because of political and financial considerations. One gets the impression that Henry VIII may have "inherited" his father's views of women in general and wives in particular.

According to an unsigned preface here, the text of this remarkable document, alluded to in Bacon's biography of Henry VII *(Item 3)*, had never before been printed.

29. **[William Tyndale].** *The practyse of Prelates. Whether the Kinges grace maye be separated from hys quene / be cause she was his brothers wyfe.* **Marborch [i.e. Antwerp: Johannes Hoochstraten], 1530.**

Tyndale is best known for his translation of the New Testament into English (1525) and it is on his translation that most subsequent translations, including the Authorized or King James Version (1611), have been based. The very act of translating Scripture into the vernacular was opposed by Cuthbert Tunstall, the bishop of London, and by the Roman Catholic Church, as it led to disputes which Rome saw as better handled by those trained in such matters, namely the Church itself. But the very availability of translations of the Bible and of reformist literature was a spur to the expansion of the Protestant Reformation. *(See Luther's* Commentary on St. Paul's Epistle to the Galatians, *Item 67).*

This book deals with two important subjects, the first being a sharp attack on the prelacy, which severely antagonized Church leaders and high government officials, such as Thomas More, as well. More important, however, in terms of this exhibition are Tyndale's aggressive objections to Henry VIII's proposed divorce of Catherine of Aragon. Distribution or reading of this book was strictly forbidden and anyone found doing so was forced to walk through London

18. Fol. D1^{R}f.

wearing the book tied on a string around the neck along with a sign proclaiming, "I have sinned against the king's laws."

The book is open to Tyndale's attack on the king's attempted divorce:

> If the kinges most noble grace will neades haue a nother wyfe / then let him serch the lawes of god / whether it be lawfull or not / for as moch as he him silf is baptized to kepethe lawes of god and hath professed them and hath sworne them. Yf the lawe of god suffre it / then let his grace put forth a litle treatyse in prynte and euen in the english tongue that all men maye se it / for his excuse and the defence of his deade and saye: Loo by the auctorite of this goddes worde do I this. And then let not his grace be a frayde ether of the emperoure / or of his lordes or of his commens & subiectes. For god hath promised to kepe them that kepe his lawes. [But, eleven pages on, Tyndale concludes] I se no remedye / but . . . a man must understond the texte thus: . . . Moses forbiddeth a man to take his brothers wife / as longe as his brother liueth: as in ye texte folowing when he forbiddeth a man to take his neyghbours wife he meaneth while his neighboure lyueth. For after his deeth it is laufull.[19]

30. H[enry] H[olland]. *Herωologia Anglica hoc est, clarissimorvm et doctissimorvm aliqovt Anglorvm qvi florvervnt ab anno Cristi M.D. vsq. ad presentem annvm MDCXX. Vivae Effigies, Vitae et elogia Duobus tomis.* Arnhem: Impensis Crispini Passaei Calcographis et Jansonij Bibliopolae Arnhemiensis, 1620.

Henry Holland, a London bookseller, published two portrait books in 1618 and 1620; the first, *Baziliωlogia,* consisted entirely of engraved portraits of English monarchs but the second, the exhibited *Herωologia,* had a good deal of letter text and a greater variety of notables: explorers, clergymen and literary figures. For many of the included subjects, these are the earliest portraits in existence.

Shown here is a portrait of Lady Jane Grey,[20] the "nine-day queen," a puppet who was executed as a result of the efforts of John Dudley, duke of Northumberland, to retain his position of power following the death of the young Edward VI; the English people showed greater loyalty to Princess Mary and the Tudor succession than to the "new religion" of Protestantism. *(See illustration, page 36.)*

19. Fol. H7^{R}ff.

20. Jane was a Protestant grandniece of Henry VIII and, of equal significance, Northumberland's daughter-in-law.

Item 30

Lady Jane Grey from Holland's *Herωologia Anglica* (1620)

31. [George Buchanan]. *Ane Detectiovn of the duinges of Marie Quene of Scottes, touchand the murder of hir husband . . . Translatit out of the Latine quhilke was written by G. B.* [London: John Day, 1571].

This volume is George Buchanan's celebrated attack on Mary, queen of Scots, a rival for the English throne and a possible successor if, as appeared quite possible, Elizabeth I were to die without issue. It charges Mary with complicity in the murder of her husband, Henry Stuart, Lord Darnley, and alleges that the so-called "Casket Letters"[21] were in her hand. Although Mary's marriage to Darnley, a great-grandson of Henry VII, had strengthened her claim to the English throne, and the birth of a son, James, solved the problem of succession to the Scottish throne and, ironically, the English throne, as well, Darnley's drunkenness and indolence were an embarrassment. Three months after Darnley's death, Mary married James Hepburn, 4th earl of Bothwell, the instigator of the murder.

George Buchanan, the author of this book, was a learned Scottish Protestant and historian. A "defamatory book by an atheist" was Mary's reaction when Elizabeth, with peculiar spite, sent her a copy when she had asked for a priest.

Note the wrapper fashioned from a late medieval French manuscript, considered unworthy of preservation.

32. [Francis Bacon]. *A Declaration of the Practises & Treasons attempted and committed by Robert late Earle of Essex and his Complices, against her Maiestie and her Kingdoms . . . Together with the very Confessions and other parts of the Euidences themselues, word for word taken out of the Originals.* London: Robert Barker, 1601.

Robert Devereux, earl of Essex, was the stepson of Robert Dudley, earl of Leicester, husband of Sir Philip Sidney's widow, son-in-law of Secretary of State Sir Francis Walsingham, a great noble and a court favorite. His temper and lofty ambition, however, were not to be controlled and eventually caused his downfall. Even early in his court

21. The "Casket Letters" were eight letters purportedly found in the possession of a retainer of James Hepburn, 4th earl of Bothwell, six days after Mary was taken prisoner by Scottish rebels in June 1567; if, as alleged, the letters were genuine and, indeed, in Mary's hand, they prove Mary's guilt in Darnley's murder.

service, Essex managed to provoke the queen's anger and, yet, somehow remain in her favor. In a dispute with Queen Elizabeth, he turned his back on her and she promptly slapped his ear. Sent as lord lieutenant to put down an Irish rebellion, he arranged an unfavorable truce, deserted his post and returned to England to explain all to his queen and try to set things aright. She, however, had had enough, stripped him of his offices and income, and subjected him to house arrest. On 8 February 1601, Essex, with 200 to 300 followers, tried to raise a popular revolt in London but this was quickly put down. He was hastily tried for treason and executed at the Tower of London on 25 February.

This is the first edition of the "official" version of the trial of the earl of Essex, written by Francis Bacon who had, in fact, been both an intermediary in Elizabeth and Essex's final disputes and a prosecutor at his trial. Bacon received £1200 from the queen as a reward for his services.[22] *(See illustration, frontispiece.)*

33. **Elizabeth I, queen of England.** *Qveene Elizabeths speech to her last parliament.* **[London: n.p.],** *c.* **1628.**

This item is one of "Gloriana's" most famous speeches, delivered approximately two months before her death and essentially her "farewell address." Here she says

> To be a King, and weare a Crown, is a thing more glorious to them that see it, then it is pleasant to them that beare it: for my selfe, I neuer was so much inticed with the glorious name of a King, or the royall authoritie of a Queene, as delighted that God hath made me His Instrument to maintaine His Truth and Glorie . . . . And though you haue had and may haue many mightier and wiser Princes sitting in this Seat, yet you neuer had nor shall haue any that will loue you better.[23]

Elizabeth had never married and the lack of a clear heir to her crown had caused a number of crises, of which those surrounding Mary, queen of Scots, are probably the most famous. It was Mary's son, King James VI of Scotland, who succeeded to the throne, as James I of England, on Elizabeth's death.

22. Lytton Strachey, *Elizabeth and Essex* (San Diego: 1956) p. 272.
23. Fol. A3^{V}ff.

34. **Charles I, king of England.** *His Majesties Declaration: To all his Loving Subjects, Of the causes which moved him to dissolve the last Parliament.* **London: Printed by Robert Barker . . . and by the assignes of John Bill, 1640.**

King Charles, having sent an army northward in an abortive campaign intended to impose the Anglican liturgy on the Scots, called the first parliament in eleven years to grant the subsidies needed for a second attack. When parliament refused his requests and scheduled a discussion of its complaints and a debate on the Scottish question, the king responded by dissolving parliament after it had sat for only three weeks. The imposed adjournment of the "Short Parliament" further strengthened opposition to the king's peremptory attitude and was one of the grievances that led to Charles's deposition and execution.

This volume is the report of the dissolution of the Short Parliament. Prior to Charles's speech, itself, it contains the official rationale for the king's powers in the matter; we can see his imperious manner on pages one and two, where it is argued that "the Calling, Adjourning, Proroguing, and Dissolving of Parliaments, are undoubted Prerogatives inseparably annexed to his Imperiall Crown, of which he is not bound to render any account but to God alone, no more then of his other Regall actions."[24]

35. **Charles I, king of England.** *ΒΑΣΙΛΙΚΑ: The Works of King Charles the Martyr* . . . . **London: Ric. Chiswell, 1687.**

This is the second edition of *Basilike*, containing the papers of Charles I "concerning the Differences betwixt His said Majesty and His Two Houses of Parliament . . . [including] His Tryal and Martyrdome." On page 173 is the king's message to parliament on 5 July 1641, in which he follows a listing of his various actions with "I have given way to every thing that you have asked of Me; and therefore Me thinks you should not wonder if in some things I begin to refuse."

---

24. Charles's continuing insistence that parliament was subject to the king, and not vice versa, was clear at his trial for treason in 1649 when he refused to argue the merits of parliament's case and dealt only with its authority to try an anointed king.

36. J[ohn] M[ilton]. *The Tenure of Kings and Magistrates: Proving That it is Lawfull . . . for any, who have the Power, to call to account a Tyrant, or wicked King, and after due conviction, to depose, and put him to death . . . .* **London: M. Simmons, 1649.**

In addition to being the author of *Paradise Lost* and other poetical works, John Milton wrote extensively on governmental matters and was deeply involved in Commonwealth politics. Within two weeks of the execution of King Charles I, Milton had composed and published this volume, the Commonwealth government's official declaration on the affair. In it he expounded the doctrine that power resides always in the people, who delegate it to a sovereign but may, if it is abused, resume it and depose or even execute the tyrant. In this work, Milton dealt with his subject only on a theoretical basis, and the deposed king was never mentioned by name; but, in an England torn by civil war and the execution of its monarch, everyone understood his point.

After the restoration of the Stuart monarchy in 1660, it became a treasonable offense to possess the text of this work, and it did not reappear in collections of Milton's writings until 1806.

37. [John Vicars]. *Former Ages Never Heard Of, and After Ages Will Admire. Or, A Brief Review of the most Materiall Parliamentary Transactions, Beginning, November 3. 1640.* **London: Printed by M.S. for Tho: Jenner, 1656.**

The title page of this small volume describes it well: "For Information of such as are altogether ignorant of the rise and progresse of these Times. A Work worthy to be kept in Record, and communicated to Posterity." It is not a great work of history but, rather, a summary of events for a public lacking easy access to the period's newspapers and pamphlets which were both fragile and quickly outdated. Particularly appealing today are the thirteen rather naïve engravings printed—with generally unsuccessful registration—within the text.

Opened to the illustration of the Coronation of Charles II, in exile, on 1 January 1651 (1650 old style).[25]

25. P. 49.

38. *Anno Regni Caroli IJ . . . At the Parliament begun at Westminster . . . [25 April 1660] . . . .* **London: Printed by John Bill and Christopher Barker, 1660.**

This book binds, in one volume, the acts of the first parliament following the restoration of Charles II in 1660; indeed, parliament began prior to Charles's actual return to London, on his thirtieth birthday, 29 May 1660, "after sundry years forced extermination into Foreign parts by the most traitorous Conspiracies." Shown here is the act designating the anniversaries of that date as occasions for thanksgiving, as Charles was "new born and raised from the dead on this most joyful day." Charles modeled his court after that of King Louis XIV of France and its contrast with the sobriety of the Puritan Commonwealth earned him the sobriquet "The Merry Monarch."

39. **[John] Michael Wright.** *An Account of His Excellence Roger Earl of Castlemaine's Embassy, From His Sacred Majesty James the II^d. King of England, Scotland, France, and Ireland, &c. To His Holiness Innocent XI. . . .* **London: Printed by Tho. Snowden for the Author, 1688.**

James II, an avowed Roman Catholic, sent Castlemaine on a mission to seek the support of Pope Innocent XI in the king's continuing conflicts with his Anglican subjects, but his efforts went unrewarded; Innocent went so far as to acquiesce in James's being supplanted by the Protestant William of Orange. The frontispiece of this volume shows Castlemaine kissing the pope's toe, while cherubs bearing James's portrait float overhead; this was, of course, highly controversial in a Protestant England which still suspected, distrusted, and feared Roman Catholicism, which it coupled with foreign influence and, potentially, with being forced to choose between the mass and the stake.

40. House of Commons. *Parliamentary Debates: Official Report, Fifth Series—Volume 318. Second session of the thirty-seventh Parliament of the United Kingdom . . . 1 Edward VIII and George VI. Second volume of session 1936–7.* London: His Majesty's Stationery Office, 1937.

This volume was Edward, duke of Windsor's personal copy of the official report of his abdication as Edward VIII, and of the debate that preceded it. "After long and anxious consideration, I have determined to renounce the Throne to which I succeeded on the death of My father, and I am now communicating this, My final and irrevocable decision. . . ."[26] Prime Minister Stanley Baldwin, following the king's message, responded, "No more grave message has ever been received by Parliament and no more difficult, I may almost say repugnant, task has ever been imposed upon a Prime Minister."[27] Also in this report is George VI's announcement, a "Message from King George VI." He stated that "I have succeeded to the Throne in circumstances which are without precedent and at a moment of great personal distress. But I am resolved to do My duty . . ."[28]

41. *Royal Warrant of King George VI creating the former King Edward VIII, duke of Windsor.* Westminster: 8 March 1937.

A major area of negotiation respecting Edward's abdication was his new title; finally, "Duke of Windsor" was selected. The original and official warrant making this creation, signed by George VI, was retained among the state papers at Windsor; this elaborate copy was made especially for the new duke. It bears the pendant wax seal of King George V, attached to the warrant by a green silk ribbon and preserved in a red morocco box gilt with the royal arms. A new seal for George VI had, of course, not yet been created.

It is worth noting that the old tradition of picturing the monarch astride a horse has continued (*see the seals shown in Section I of this exhibition*); armor, however, has been abandoned for more modern attire.

---

26. Column 2175.
27. Column 2176.
28. Column 2241.

I V

Social Commentary

THE bulk of this exhibition deals with privilege and wealth: royalty, splendid occasions, magnificent buildings. Books with pictures of princes sold better than did books with pictures of paupers, and they have also been better preserved. Even so, books dealing with social issues became more numerous in the nineteenth century, as the industrial revolution further widened the gap between rich and poor. The four books comprising this part of the exhibition deal sympathetically with the problems of the lower classes, although the title of Item 44, Busby's *Costumes of the Lower Orders*, might be seen in today's world as being rather derogatory of its subjects.

42. Henry Mayhew. *London Labour and the London Poor*. London: Charles Griffen and Company, 1864. Four volumes.

This is the revised edition of Henry Mayhew's classic, the first three volumes of which were first published in 1851 and the fourth and last only in 1862. The fourth volume is rarer than the first three, having had a smaller press run due to the unsavory nature of its subjects: prostitutes, swindlers, thieves, and beggars. Mayhew was a humane journalist and sociologist, whose study of London's poor greatly influenced Dickens.

The book is unusual in that many of the illustrations in the text were engraved after photographs, rather than drawings or paintings. The street-seller depicted in the displayed illustration wears a sign: "I was born cripple," not unlike similarly afflicted poor in today's London and other urban centers.

43. Charles Dickens. *Bleak House*. London: Bradbury & Evans, 1852–53. Twenty parts in nineteen wrappers.

Bleak House (1852–53), *Hard Times* (1854), and *Little Dorrit* (1855–57) are known as Dickens's "dark novels" for their somber picture of contemporary society. In his writing Dickens often used actual characters, institutions and places as the basis for the fictionalized ones of his novels and his descriptions of poverty and hunger are among the sharpest pictures we have of the life of England's lower classes in the nineteenth century.

Bleak House was one of Dickens's novels which were published "in parts"; as with most of the others, this work was issued in twenty parts over nineteen months, the last two parts being combined into one volume. This publication format may be looked upon as a precursor of radio and television serials, although each novel had a pre-planned number of parts and didn't just run on until the audience vanished.

44. T[homas] L. Busby. *Costume of the Lower Orders of London* bound with *The Fishing Costume and Local Scenery of Hartlepool, in the County of Durham.* **London: T. L. Busby, [1820] / London: J. Nichols and Son, 1819.**

Nineteenth-century London was full of itinerant unskilled labor, such as the tinker pictured in Busby's work; others portrayed in this book include a match-girl, a mechanical fiddler, an apple-boy, a rabbit-seller, and a fortune-teller. Busby's work is unusual in that most of his illustrations were drawn from actual individuals rather than from the artist's memory or imagination.

45. [Charles Dickens]. Timothy Sparks, pseudonym. *Sunday Under Three Heads . . . .* **London: Chapman and Hall, 1836.**

The dawn of the Victorian Age was, perhaps, even more "Victorian" than it was to become in later years. Dickens, using the pseudonym "Timothy Sparks," wrote this pamphlet as a protest against the extreme views of Sir Andrew Agnew and the Sabbatarian party which had sponsored a Bill "for the better observance of the Sabbath"; this legislation had only recently and narrowly been rejected in the House of Commons.

Dickens was a strong supporter of freedom of the Sabbath for the poor man and here suggested easing, not tightening, of the Sabbath laws. Queen Victoria concurred, saying, "I am not at all an admirer or approver of our very dull Sunday."

V

Royal, Civil, and Ecclesiastical Architecture

COUNTED among the glories of England must be its castles and palaces, its public buildings, its universities and public schools, its churches and cathedrals. Included in the exhibition are five great color-plate books published in London between 1808 and 1816 by Rudolph Ackermann, covering London, Westminster Abbey, Oxford and Cambridge universities, and the English public schools. The collection exhibited here originally was focused on books about London, especially its topography, and books illustrating its wonderful buildings remain a core area.

Royal Residences and Government Buildings

46. *The Microcosm of London.* London: R. Ackermann's Repository of Arts, 1808–10. Three volumes.

Ackermann's splendid book contains 104 hand-colored aquatint views of London and represents the marriage of two huge talents, the architecture having been drawn by Augustus Pugin and the human figures by Thomas Rowlandson. A leading author on color-plate books wrote, "The 'Microcosm of London' is one of the great colour-plate books, and a carefully selected copy should form the corner stone of any collection of books on this subject. The plates by Rowlandson and Pugin present an unrivalled picture of London in early nineteenth century, of historic value, as many of the buildings no longer exist."[29] And, from an early twentieth-century author on the art of aquatinting: "the book is a perfect treasure-house of scenes, described with pen and brush, from the London of a century ago, the work of Rowlandson and Pugin being equally admirable."[30]

Shown here is the plate depicting Westminster Hall, which was built in 1097 as an extension to Edward the Confessor's Palace of Westminster, of which it is the only surviving part. The Hall was

---

29. R. V. Tooley, *English Books with Coloured Plates 1790–1860* (London: 1987) p. 22.

30. S. T. Prideaux, *Aquatint Engraving* (London: 1909) p. 123.

restored by Edward II after a fire in 1291 and additional alterations were made by Richard II in 1397–99. The oak hammer-beam roof is the largest unsupported span in England, although steel reinforcement was added in 1920.

47. **W. H. Pyne. *The History of the Royal Residences* . . . . London: A. Dry, 1819. Three volumes.**

This volume contains one hundred hand-colored aquatint etchings and also bound in are uncolored impressions of sixty-four subjects; of the latter, sixty-one are duplicates of published plates but three others are not included in the book, as published. Illustrations of the interiors of the various royal homes are particularly striking for their attention to detail. However, "this set of plates could not hope to equal in popularity Ackermann's *Microcosm (Item 46)* since there could only be a limited public for a series consisting chiefly of well-upholstered palace interiors peopled only by the occasional decorous gentlemen or lady in waiting, or obsequious flunkeys and innumerable oil paintings—a far cry from Rowlandson's Billingsgate fishwives, Covent-Garden bully-boys and St. James's macaronis."[31]
The plate shown here depicts the chapel of Hampton Court Palace which is not, strictly speaking, royal architecture, having been built by Cardinal Thomas Wolsey. Wolsey "presented" it, under considerable pressure, to Henry VIII, who could not abide his subordinate's ostentatious display of wealth and power. Five of Henry's six wives lived in Hampton Court Palace; his third wife, Jane Seymour, died there after giving birth to Henry's only legitimate surviving son, Edward VI; Queen Mary lived there for four years, hoping, in vain, for a child; Elizabeth I, James I, Charles I, and William & Mary also made it their home during part of their reigns.

48. ***Londina Illustrata; Graphic And Historic Memorials of Monasteries, Churches, Chapels, Schools, Charitable Foundations, Palaces, Halls, Courts, Processions, Places of Early Amusement and Modern & Present Theatres, in the Cities and Suburbs of London & Westminster.* London: Robert Wilkinson, 1819. Two volumes.**

Londina Illustrata is particularly important as the record of many of the lesser buildings of London, such as theaters, almshouses, and private homes, which have long since been destroyed. Extremely

31. Adams, *London Illustrated*, p. 324.

complicated bibliographically, with many variants,[32] this copy, a large paper set with superb contemporary hand-coloring, contains many more plates (164) than necessary (127), but fewer than the later edition of 1834 (206).

The plate shown here is that of Somerset House, England's first Renaissance palace, built in 1547–50 in the Strand for Edward Seymour, duke of Somerset, lord protector and uncle of Edward VI. Following Somerset's execution in 1552, the house was forfeited to the crown and was occupied occasionally by Princess Elizabeth; she rode out from here the following year to welcome her half-sister, Mary, to London as England's new queen. Later, it was occupied by the consorts of James I, Charles I, and Charles II. Somerset House was demolished in the late eighteenth century and on its site was built England's first large government office building, still in use today.

Note the boat arriving at the entrance facing London's main thoroughfare, the River Thames.

49. Thomas Shotter Boys, artist. *Original Views of London As It Is . . . with Historical and Descriptive Notices . . . by Charles Ollier.* London: Thomas Boys, 1842.

This book consists of twenty-six hand-colored tinted lithographs and a lithographed dedication leaf; each plate is accompanied by a letterpress leaf of text. In many ways, Boys's *London As It Is* gives us a record of the London of the 1840s as Ackermann's *Microcosm (Item 46)* did for the period some thirty years earlier. As Bernard Adams pointed out, Boys's illustrations "are well drawn and . . . suitable to their settings. Their attitudes, where not elegant, are usually quite relaxed in great contrast to the multifarious and almost maniacal activity of the human beings introduced at times by Rowlandson into the *Microcosm* plates."[33] The facsimile edition published by Charles Traylen in 1954 is far less attractive than the handcolored aquatints of the original.

Today's visitor to London might encounter ladies (in more modern attire) walking their dogs in front of St. James's Palace, at the

32. The 1819 edition usually carries 127 plates. However, a correct collation for this work is almost impossible, since, at his death in 1825, all Wilkinson's materials for *Londina Illustrata* were sold by Sotheby's to Gale, who then bound them up, thus creating a host of variants and adding considerably to the already complex evolution of this work.

33. Adams, *London Illustrated*, p. 469.

same spot as illustrated here, but nursemaids carrying and leading their charges certainly wouldn't be chatting with a sentry!

50. H[umphrey] Repton. *Designs for the Pavillon at Brighton.* **London: J. C. Stadler, 1808.**

In 1805, the Prince of Wales (later George IV) asked Humphrey Repton, a professional landscape designer, for his advice on the re-design and rebuilding of the Brighton Pavilion, a royal residence on the Channel coast. Repton's successful career had been due not only to his keen judgment and expertise in garden layout but also to his practice of making watercolor drawings of the grounds to be rebuilt, with an overlay showing his proposed alterations.

His proposal is reflected in this volume which contains twenty plates and vignettes including a hand-colored General Ground Plan. Shown here is "The General View from the Pavillon" with the "before and after" flaps of paper that were a hallmark of Repton's works.

Lack of funds prevented Repton's landscape designs from being carried out and those of John Nash, the architect of Buckingham Palace, were incorporated in the 1824 rebuilding of the Pavilion. *(See Item 51.)* Repton claimed, not without reason, that Nash had stolen his idea of using an Indian architectural style for the Royal Pavilion.

51. *Sickelmores' Select Views of Brighton.* **Brighton: C. and R. Sickelmore, [n.d., ca. 1827].**

Nine views of Brighton are illustrated in this lovely volume; shown here is the Brighton Pavilion, rebuilt by John Nash (who also developed London's Regent Street and Regent's Park, and also was the architect of Buckingham Palace) as a retreat for George, Prince of Wales and regent for his father, George III. The reconstruction was accomplished, at enormous cost, with a fanciful Indian exterior, in recognition of England's growing empire.

Schools and Colleges

52. Dav[id] Loggan. *Oxonia Illustrata* . . . . **Oxford: Sheldonian Theatre, 1675.**

Other than preliminaries, there is no text in this handsome volume, only "justly celebrated views"[34] which are "a notable example of Loggan's accurate but rather stiff draughts-manship."[35] The three-leaf view of Christ Church College is shown here.

Christ Church was founded as Cardinal College in 1525 by Cardinal Thomas Wolsey, utilizing the proceeds and income stemming from the dissolution of twenty-two religious houses, for which he had received a bull from Pope Clement VII. Following the cardinal's downfall, the college was refounded by Henry VIII as Christ Church.

This plate, dated 1673, includes the still unfinished entrance tower. *(See Item 53.)*

✳ ✳ ✳ ✳

From 1814 to 1816, Rudolph Ackermann, the renowned publisher, issued three of his most important books of hand-colored aquatints. Covering Oxford and Cambridge universities and also a number of the English public (private) schools, these volumes provide the best record of these famous educational institutions as they appeared in the early nineteenth century.

53. *A History of the University of Oxford* . . . . **London: R. Ackermann, 1814. Two volumes.**

Ackermann's plate shows Christ Church's gate 140 years after the Loggan view *(Item 52)*. The great entrance tower, which neither Wolsey nor Henry VIII finished, had been completed in 1682 to Christopher Wren's design. Referring to this item and to Ackermann's *Cambridge (Item 54)*, Prideaux wrote that "these two books are among the finest ever executed. . . . [the drawings] by A[ugustus] Pugin, F[rederick] Nash, F[rederick] Mackenzie, and W[illiam]

34. Falconer Maden, *Oxford Books* (Oxford: 1931) vol. III, p. 308.
35. Nicolas Barker, *Treasures from the Libraries of National Trust Country Houses* (New York: 1999) p. 56.

Item 54

King's College Chapel from Ackermann's *Cambridge* (1815)

Westall are worthy even of the splendid architectural monuments they commemorate, [and are] plates of unequalled merit in their particular line."[36]

54. *A History of the University of Cambridge* .... London: R. Ackermann, 1815. Two volumes.

The second of Ackermann's three works on English educational institutions, on the University of Cambridge, includes a portrait of the dedicatee, sixty-four hand-colored aquatint plates drawn primarily by Pugin, Mackenzie, and Westall, and fifteen costume plates drawn by Thomas Uwins, in addition to extensive text.

King's College, Cambridge was founded by Henry VI in 1441 to provide a college for graduates of his recently founded school at Eton. Construction of the renowned chapel commenced in 1446 but was suspended during the Wars of the Roses, proceeded under Edward IV and Henry VII, and was finished only under Henry VIII, some hundred years after it was begun. Twenty-five of the chapel's windows still have their original glass, a very special treasure as most of England's medieval stained glass was destroyed during the Reformation and Protectorate. The nave and choir vault was built between 1512 and 1515, with fan vaulting somewhat less elaborate than that in the Henry VII Chapel in Westminster Abbey *(see Items 58 and 59).* *(See illustration, facing page.)*

55. *The History of the Colleges of Winchester, Eton, and Westminster* .... London: R. Ackermann, 1816.

Ackermann's volume contains views of the nine principal public schools, with more plates of the most prestigious than the least (Eton and Winchester have ten each; St. Paul's and Merchant Taylors' each have only two). The publisher employed seven artists for this book, primarily Pugin, Mackenzie, and Westall. Ackermann's expectation that this would be a popular work, appealing to alumni of the nine schools, was apparently misguided; sales lagged and the remaining sheets were eventually issued in separate folios for each school.

The plate exhibited, William Westall's drawing depicting Charterhouse from its playground, is in its second state. In its first state there were two washerwomen laying out linen on the lawn with eleven

36. Prideaux, *Aquatint Engraving,* p. 126.

other figures on the paths; the plate was redone, following objections that depicting the washerwomen was offensive, substituting thirteen boys and masters playing cricket.

Ecclesiastical Architecture

56. Joseph Nash. *Architecture of the Middle Ages*. London: T. Maclean, 1838.

Joseph Nash (1808–78) was primarily an architectural draftsman, who began his training under A. C. Pugin. His "large lithographed books of picturesque architecture which appeared in the 1830s and 1840s . . . are still regarded as the most accurate views of medieval houses and castles. Nash's figures . . . brought the buildings to life, without detracting from the serious antiquarianism of the book."[37] The plates of *Architecture of the Middle Ages*, in addition to houses and castles, illustrate the exteriors and interiors of ecclesiastical buildings in England (Oxford, Winchester, Arundel, etc.), as well as in continental Europe.

The exhibited illustration of Winchester Cathedral is from what is possibly a unique copy of Nash's first book with a pictorial title and twenty-five lithographed plates, all hand-colored by Nash, mounted as drawings on thick cards. Each mount is captioned in pencil and signed by the artist in ink.

The glory of the historic city of Winchester is its great cathedral, the longest (556 feet [169 meters]) in England. The original Saxon Cathedral Church of St. Swithun was replaced by the Norman structure of Bishop Walkelin (1070–98); the nave was rebuilt in the Perpendicular Gothic style in the fourteenth century under two great bishops, William of Edington and William of Wykeham. The cathedral has required extensive twentieth-century restoration, including underpinning of its insecure foundations. *(See illustration, facing page.)*

Westminster Abbey

Utilizing the site of an old Benedictine monastery, Edward the Confessor built a new, large cruciform church which was consecrated in 1065, only months before the great Norman invasion. Edward III, in

---

37. Simon Houfe, *Dictionary of British Book Illustrators and Caricaturists 1800–1914* ([N.P.]: 1981) p. 397.

Item 56

Winchester Cathedral from Nash's *Architecture of the Middle Ages* (1838)

1245, destroyed all but the nave of Edward's church and built a new church in the Gothic style of his day; the nave, itself, was rebuilt in Gothic, over many years, starting in 1376. Although commonly known as "Westminster Abbey," the church's proper designation is the "Collegiate Church of St. Peter in Westminster," the name it was given at its refounding by Elizabeth I in 1560.

All British sovereigns since William the Conqueror (1066) have been crowned in the abbey, except Edward V and Edward VIII, neither of whom was ever crowned. The abbey is crowded with tombs *(see Item 57)* of royalty, many of whom are buried near Edward the Confessor's shrine or in Henry VII's magnificent chapel *(see Items 58 and 59)*, and those of commoners whose tombs occupy the transepts and a good portion of the nave and aisles.

57. **[William Camden].** *Reges, Reginae, Nobiles, & alij in Ecclesia Collegiata B. Petri Westmonasterij sepulti, vsque ad Annum reparat & salutis 1600.* **London: E. Bollifant, 1600.**

This small volume is the first edition of the first guide to Westminster Abbey's epitaphs. It is open to the description of the tombs of Henry VII and his wife, Elizabeth of York, which are situated, appropriately, in the Henry VII Chapel. *(See Items 58 and 59.)*

58. *The History of the Abbey Church of St. Peter's Westminster . . . .* **London: R. Ackermann, 1812. Two volumes.**

The illustrations to Ackermann's *Westminster Abbey* consist of a portrait of the dedicatee, a plan, and eighty-two additional hand-colored aquatint plates, drawn primarily by Augustus Pugin and Frederick Mackenzie. It was intended as a continuation of the *Microcosm (see Item 46)*, utilizing many of the same artists, engravers, and authors, although it does not achieve the full magnificence or charm of the earlier work.

Exhibited here is the plate depicting Henry VII's majestic perpendicular Gothic chapel. It was originally intended as a shrine to the saintly King Henry VI but, when the latter's canonization failed, the chapel became a memorial to its benefactor, Henry VII, himself. The glorious fan vaulting is unique to the English Gothic architectural style. *(See Item 54.)*

59. A. L. Rowse, John Betjeman, George Zarnecki, John Pope-Hennessy, *et al. Westminster Abbey.* Radnor, PA: The Annenberg School Press, 1972.

Walter Annenberg, U.S. ambassador to the Court of St. James, who financed this handsome volume, intended it to be the twentieth-century equivalent of Ackermann's *Westminster Abbey*, Item 58 in this exhibition. The photograph of the fan vaulting of the Henry VII Chapel provides a handsome complement to Ackermann's aquatint illustration.

St. Paul's Cathedral

IN 1658, William Dugdale published his *History of St. Paul's Cathedral.* This was not the cathedral we know today, but "Old St. Paul's," a gothic structure that had been ravaged by time and weather, not to mention Cromwell's troops and horses who had been quartered there during the Civil War. Dugdale's *History* was extremely detailed, with plates by the leading engraver of the day, Wenceslaus Hollar, covering every possible aspect of the old church. Following the Restoration in 1660, a committee, including one Christopher Wren, was established to consider shoring up and rebuilding Old St. Paul's. The cathedral burned to the ground, however, in the Great Fire of 1666, and Wren was appointed to design for London a new, magnificent cathedral, suited to its position as one of the world's leading cities.

60. William Dugdale. *The History of S[t.] Pauls Cathedral* . . . . London: Tho[mas] Warren, 1658.

"The importance of this book for London topography lies not so much in Dugdale's learned transcriptions, cataloguings and comments as in the magnificent plates by [Wenceslaus] Hollar which illustrate them. Thanks to these it is the first printed book to delineate in considerable detail an English building. . . . It is an accurate graphic record of that fortunately unique phenomenon, an English Gothic cathedral which was to be reduced to rubble."[38] For John Aubrey, the seventeenth-century antiquarian and writer, "that

38. Adams, *London Illustrated,* pp. 14–15.

stupendous fabric of Paul's Church, not a stone left on stone, . . . lives now only in Mr. Hollar's etchings."[39]

Although this cathedral is known as "Old St. Paul's," it is not the first church built on this site; indeed, a church which was destroyed by fire in 1087 was built, according to legend supported by a good deal of physical evidence, on the site of a Roman temple dedicated to Diana. Started promptly following the devastating 1087 fire, "Old St. Paul's" was largely completed by 1340; it differed, however, from Hollar's St. Paul's in that there had been changes following the 1340 completion: for example, the immense timber spire, which towered 124 feet higher than the present cathedral's dome, had been struck by lightning and never replaced. After Charles II's restoration (1660), a committee, including Christopher Wren, a young mathematician/architect/professor of astronomy, was formed to plan the rebuilding of St. Paul's, but this was never accomplished. Following the cathedral's complete destruction in London's Great Fire (1666), Wren designed the present St. Paul's Cathedral, now a major London landmark, as a site for Protestant ceremony. *(See Item 63, Wren's plan for rebuilding post-fire London.)*

This volume belonged to Sir Christopher Wren and bears his signature on the title page. *(See illustration, facing page.)*

61. H[enry] H[olland]. *Monvmenta Sepvlchraria Sancti Pavli: The Monvments, Inscriptions, and Epitaphs, of Kings, Nobles, Bishops, and others, buried in the Cathedrall Church of S^t. Pavl, London. Untill this present yeere of Grace, 1614 . . . Never before, now with authoritie, published.* **London: [Eliot's Court Press] for Matthew Law and H. Holland, [1614].**

This book provides an invaluable record of the inscriptions and funeral monuments of Old St. Paul's, monuments which were destroyed in the Great Fire of London. At the beginning is a short chapter on the foundation of St. Paul's, and at the end a list of the bishops of London.

The book is opened to the acrostic epitaph for Sir Francis Walsingham, principal secretary to Queen Elizabeth I.[40] A devout Protestant, Walsingham considered Catholic Spain to be England's worst enemy; he established what was, in essence, England's first "Secret

39. John Aubrey, quoted in Anthony Powell, *John Aubrey and His Friends* (London: 1948) p. 273, cited by Rachel Doggett et al., *Impressions of Wenceslaus Hollar* (Washington: 1996) p. 43.

40. Fol. C3^V f.

THE
HISTORY
OF
S.t PAULS CATHEDRAL
IN
LONDON,

From its Foundation untill thefe Times:

Extracted out of { Originall CHARTERS.
RECORDS.
LEIGER BOOKS, and other
MANUSCRIPTS.

Beautified with fundry Profpects of the Church,
Figures of Tombes, and Monuments.

By *WILLIAM DVGDALE.*

Pfalm. 48. 12, 13.

*Walke about Sion, and go round about her ; tell the
Towers thereof : Marke ye well her Bulwarks, confider her
Palaces, that ye may tell it to the Generations following.*

Tibullus.

*Non ego, fi merui, dubitem procumbere Templis,
Et dare facratis ofcula liminibus.*

London, Printed by *Tho. Warren*, in the year
of our Lord God MDCLVIII.

Item 60

Christopher Wren's copy of Dugdale's *History
of S.t Paul's Cathedral* (title page) (1658)

Service," and he spent much of his career seeking out and frustrating conspiracies against his monarch's life.

62. William Dugdale, ed. Henry Ellis. *The History of Saint Paul's Cathedral . . . With a Continuation and Additions . . . .* London: Lackington, Hughes, Harding, Mavor, and Jones *and* Longman, Hurst, Reese, Orme, and Brown, 1818.

Most copies of Dugdale's 1658 edition *(Item 60)* were undoubtedly lost in the Great Fire and no new edition of his work was published after 1716 until this handsome issue of 1818. This third edition provides a complete description of Wren's seventeenth-century masterpiece, in addition to reproducing the 1658 material. Bernard Adams, in his important *London Illustrated: 1604–1851*, commented that "these plates are extraordinary examples of facsimile work, the measurements being correct to within a millimetre; had [William Finden] substituted Hollar's credit for his own and engraved the dedication cartouches and original captions, and had the etchings been printed on laid paper, they would have deceived all but the expert."[41]

Shown here is Finden's re-engraving of Hollar's plate of Old St. Paul's as viewed from the north.

63. Christopher Wren. *A Plan of the City of London, after the great Fire in the Year of Our Lord 1666, with the Modell of the New City, according to the Design and Proposal of S! Christopher Wren K! &c. . . . . .* [N.P.: n.p.], 1744.

Christopher Wren, as royal architect, produced a plan in 1666 for the rebuilding of London after the Great Fire, but it, like others from many prominent designers, was not adopted. Churchill wrote that "to later times it seems that the great calamity [of the Fire] was not so much the destruction of the insanitary medieval city as the failure to carry through Wren's plan for rebuilding it as a unit of quays and avenues centred on St Paul's and the Royal Exchange."[42]

As one would expect, a new St. Paul's Cathedral occupied a prominent place, as had the recently destroyed cathedral. Wren had not, at this time, designed the new St. Paul's; note that the "generic"

41. Adams, *London Illustrated* p. 288.
42. Churchill, *The New World* p. 348.

cathedral represented on the plan included a dome in the classical style, as had Wren's proposal for the renovation of Old St. Paul's, as well as his final design for its replacement.

64. **John Stow.** *A Survey of The Cities of London and Westminster, and the Borough of Southwark* . . . . **London: W. Innys and J. Richardson, etc., 1754–55 [57]. Two volumes.**

Stow's *Survey* was first published in 1598; this is the sixth edition, "corrected, improved, and very much enlarged by John Strype." It is a virtual walking tour of old London with meticulous description and 132[43] maps and plates of almost every detail of the city's geography, buildings, and monuments.[44]

The book is opened at the double-page engraving of Wren's classic St. Paul's Cathedral, as seen from the northwest. It appeared much as it is today, but without the crowds and traffic. As evidence of the detail in Stow and Strype's work, note the various dimensions of St. Paul's in the second column of the visible text.

43. This copy lacks one of the 132 plates.
44. For a charming, imaginary "perambulation" through Tudor London, with John Stow as your guide, see Walter Besant's *London* (New York: 1892) pp. 320–370.

V I

The English Reformation

THE sixteenth-century Protestant Reformation in England differed greatly from that on the continent of Europe. Whereas in Europe the teachings of Martin Luther, John Calvin, and others found a receptive audience within a disaffected Roman Catholic population, the English Reformation was more "top-down." That is, the break with Rome came about, less from differences in theology or ecclesiology, but more because Henry VIII needed to find a solution to the "king's great matter." The solution was found only by declaring independence from the Roman Catholic Church and was imposed on a populace that recent scholarship suggests was not entirely enthusiastic about embracing the "new religion,"[45] even though it saw the Church as thoroughly corrupt. In addition, of course, the dissolution of the monasteries provided the crown much additional wealth for the king to retain for income or distribute to courtiers.

Henry, himself, was essentially a religious conservative and it was only after his death that Protestantism became firmly entrenched in England. Indeed, the king had received his title "Defender of the Faith" from a grateful Pope Leo X for his attack on Martin Luther and his teachings; not only did he find Luther repugnant theologically, but the reformer's advocacy of a "priesthood of all believers," in its threats to the papacy, threatened temporal authority as well. In the final analysis, as Professor Scarisbrick said it best, "Henry's religion could be moulded to any shape, as prestige, profit and power required. To few men did religion matter more than to Henry; but probably mainly because he could melt down the things that were God's and so easily imprint his own image on the newly-minted coin."[46]

Protestantism flourished under Henry's son, Edward VI,[47] who in his minority was controlled by two Protestant protectors, but it foundered under the obsessive Roman Catholic Mary I, during whose reign Protestants were subject to severe persecution. It was only with the accession of Elizabeth I that a middle ground, a form of Catholicism without the pope, became

---

45. See Eamon Duffy, *The Stripping of the Altars: Traditional Religion in England c. 1400–c.1580* (New Haven and London: 1992).

46. J. J. Scarisbrick, *Henry VIII* (Berkeley and Los Angeles: 1968) p. 417.

47. Professor G. R. Elton, in *Reform and Reformation: England 1509–1558* (Cambridge, MA: 1977) p. 354, colorfully described Edward's Protestantism as "an uncompromising bigotry very characteristic of the newly converted adolescent."

the form of the Church of England. Yet the Puritans, who wanted to "purify" the Church of its remnants of Roman practice, kept the religious pot boiling for many years.

Nowhere was the aphorism, *cuius regio, eius religio* (whose territory, his religion), more appropriate than in Tudor England, from the orthodox Roman Catholicism of Henry VII, to the wavering orthodoxy and rejection of papal authority of Henry VIII, to Protestantism under Edward VI, to the return of Roman Catholicism under Mary and, finally, to the *via media* of the Elizabethan Settlement.

65. [Desiderius] Erasmus. *In Evangelivm Lvcae Paraphrasis Erasmi Roterodami nunc primum & nata & aedita.* Basel: Joan. Frob[en], 1523.

Erasmus's *Paraphrase of St. Luke* went through some fifteen printings before 1550; the exhibited copy is the first edition, published in Basel by Erasmus's friend, printer, and publisher, Johann Froben. "Paraphrase is sometimes the best form of commentary. Erasmus was not content with the simple, more or less factual annotation of the New Testament, but went on to paraphrase, which enabled him to soar higher and to dig deeper. His paraphrases had the advantage of being a comparatively new form when they were written, and they were so well-liked and became so popular that edition after edition was called for during his lifetime and after his death. King Edward VI of England went so far as to decree that a copy should be placed beside the Bible in every parish church in his realm."[48] Shown is the opening of the *Paraphrase of St. Luke's* long dedication to Henry VIII, who in 1521 had been named "Defender of the Faith" by Pope Leo X as a reward for the king's pamphlet *Assertio septem sacramentorum aduersus Martinum Lutherum* (*"Assertion of the Seven Sacraments Against Martin Luther"*).

Erasmus was both a theological conservative and a critic of ecclesiastical abuses, making him a target of suspicion for adherents to both sides of the reformation controversies. He took a strong position in favor of biblical translation into vernacular languages; in the "Exhortation" with which he prefaced his new Latin translation of the New Testament, he wrote: "I totally dissent from those who are unwilling that the sacred Scriptures, translated in the vulgar tongue, should be read by private individuals. I would wish even all women

48. James E. Walsh, *Erasmus on the 500th anniversary of his birth* [the catalogue of the Houghton Library Erasmus quincentenary exhibition] (Cambridge, Massachusetts: 1969) p. 23.

to read the Gospel, and the Epistles of St. Paul. I wish they were translated into all languages of the people. I wish that the husbandman might sing parts of them at his plough, and the weaver at his shuttle, and that the traveller might beguile with their narration the weariness of his way."[49]

The book is interesting also for its contemporary English binding of blind-stamped calf over wooden boards. On the upper cover panel is a miller on a donkey with a sack of flour over his shoulder and the signature of the binder, Johan Moulin; on the lower cover panel is a miller climbing down a ladder from a windmill. The volume has been rebacked, preserving most of the original spine, and has pastedowns from a medieval manuscript.

66. [Richard] Rolt. *The Lives of the Principal Reformers, Both Englishmen and Foreigners. Comprehending the General History of the Reformation; From its Beginning, in 1360, by Dr. John Wickliffe, To its Establishment, in 1600, under Queen Elizabeth. With an Introduction; wherein The Reformation is amply vindicated, and its Necessity fully shewn, from the Degeneracy of the Clergy, and the Tyranny of the Popes. By Mr. Rolt. The Whole embellished with the Heads of the Reformers, Elegantly done in Metzotinto, by Mr. Houston.* **London: Printed for E. Bakewell and H. Parker; J. Robinson; and T. Pote, 1759.**

The text of this history, while interesting, is undistinguished; Richard Houston's twenty-one mezzotints of the reformers are, however, lovely. They include not only the usual continentals: Luther, Zwingli, Calvin, etc., but also many of those important principally to the English Reformation: Henry VIII, Edward VI, Elizabeth I, Cranmer, Latimer, Ridley, Hooper, etc.

The book is open to a portrait of Thomas Cranmer who, as a scholar and theologian, became heavily involved in Henry VIII's "great matter," the divorce from Catherine of Aragon; his was the suggestion that the theological question be referred to the universities of England and Europe, a jury likely to respond favorably to Henry. Chosen by the king to become the archbishop of Canterbury, he did as he was expected to, declaring that Henry and Catherine's marriage was void from its inception and that Henry and Anne Boleyn were, indeed, legally married.

---

49. Cited by H. W. Hoare, *The Evolution of the English Bible* (London: 1901) p. 113.

An innovative theologian, Cranmer, through his writing and preaching *(Items 69, 71, 72, 74)*, strongly influenced England's conversion to Protestantism. He suffered a heretic's death by burning in 1556, during the reign of Queen Mary, thrusting his right hand, with which he had signed a recantation of his Protestantism, into the flames so it would burn first.

Diarmaid MacCulloch, in his monumental biography, credited Cranmer with the first use (1535) of the term "reformation" as applied to the changes taking place in the Church. "Cranmer had innocently hit on a term that would resound through later historical writing, although it does not seem to have been generally taken up at the time."[50]

67. **Martin Luther.** *A Commentarie of M. Doctor Martin Lvther vpon the Epistle of S. Paul to the Galathians, first collected and gathered vvord by vvord out of his preaching, and novv out of Latine faithfully translated into English for the vnlearned* . . . . **London: Thomas Vautroullier, 1575.**

First published in Latin in 1535, this is the first edition in English of one of Luther's most important and influential biblical commentaries. In his spiritual autobiography, *Grace Abounding to the Chief of Sinners,* John Bunyan wrote that he preferred this book before all others except the Bible as "most fit for a wounded conscience."

In a preface commending the book "To the Reader," the bishop of London, Edwin Sandys, called the doctrine of salvation by faith "this most necessarye doctrine [which] the author hath most substantially cleared in this his comment. Which being written in the Latine tounge, certaine godly learned men haue most sincerely translated into our language, to the great benefite of all such as with humbled hartes wil diligently reade the same."[51]

68. *Hor[a]e Beatissime virginis marie ad legitimum Sarisburiensis Ecclesie ritum cum quindecim orationibus beate Brigitte* . . . . **[Paris: Francis Regnault], 1534.**

". . . the Primer was a Layman's book of devotions for private use either at home or in church; to prove this it is enough to quote some rubrics to the Latin prayers, such for instance as, 'Ere ye depart out

---

50. Diarmaid MacCulloch, *Thomas Cranmer: A Life* (New York and London: 1996) p. 142.
51. Fol. *ii.

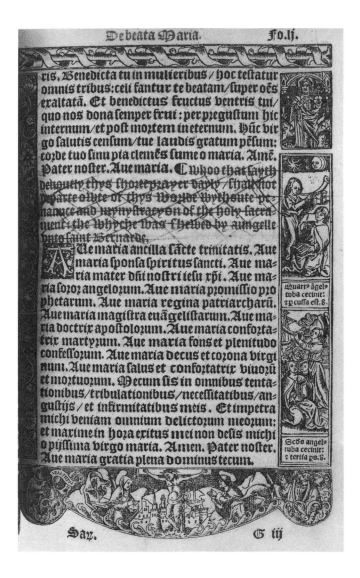

Item 68

Book of Hours with contemporary inked deletions (1534)

of your chamber at your uprising,' 'when thou enterest into the church,' 'when thou shalt receive the sacrament.' "[52] The great majority of this book's rubrics are in English, as are the "forme of confessyon," the ten commandments, the fifteen "Os," and many of the descriptive verses accompanying illustrations. Published in 1534 in Paris for the English market, the woodcut designs include the arms of England, the shield with three Tudor roses, and St. George.

In addition, 1534 was the year of enactment of the Act of Succession (25 Hen. 8, c. 22.) and the Act of Supremacy (26 Hen. 8, c. 1.); under the latter the king was recognized as "supreme head of the Church of England." In this copy, many of the rubrics which are particularly offensive to anti-Romans have been crossed out in ink, but this has been lightly done and they are still legible; in several cases the word "pope" has been scraped. In the Pierpont Morgan Library copy there are fewer inked excisions but more scraping than in this volume. The book is very rare; in addition to the present and Morgan Library copies, STC[53] shows only two copies in America. *(See illustration, page 65.)*

69. *The Institvtion of a Christen Man, conteynynge the Exposytion or Interpretation of the commune Crede, of the seuen Sacramentes . . . .* **(Commonly known as** *The Bishops' Book.***) London: Thomas Berthelet, 1537.**

Written by a group of twenty-one bishops (headed by the liberal Thomas Cranmer) and twenty-five other lawyers and ecclesiastics (including the conservative Edmund Bonner, then archdeacon of Leicester, later, in the reign of the Catholic Mary I, bishop of London), this was meant to be a definitive statement of faith, fully approved by King Henry VIII. While historians A. G. Dickens and G. R. Elton both saw it as essentially defending Catholic orthodoxy, it strays from orthodoxy in critical areas: for example, there is no mention of transubstantiation, key to the Roman Catholic faith; it clearly permits the Protestant doctrine of justification by faith alone; and it deals with prayer for departed souls by suggesting that its usefulness is uncertain, at best. In the end, Henry never gave *The Bishops' Book*

---

52. Edgar Hoskins, *Horae Beatae Mariae Virginis or Sarum and York Primers with kindred books and Primers of the Reformed Roman Use together with an introduction . . .* (New York: 1901) p. xv.

53. A. W. Pollard & G. R. Redgrave, *A Short-Title Catalogue of Books Printed in England, Scotland & Ireland and of English Books Printed Abroad: 1475–1640: Second Edition, revised and enlarged . . . by W. A. Jackson, F. S. Ferguson . . . [and] Katharine F. Pantzer* (London: 1976–91), three volumes.

his stamp of approval, claiming lack of time to consider the matter. When it was revised in 1543 to conform with Henry's demands, the new book became known, not as the second edition of *The Bishops' Book* but, appropriately, as *The King's Book (Item 70)*. In addition to this copy, the STC shows only four copies in America, one of which is imperfect.

Note the (? first owner's) inscription on the title page:

"Ann° Dm 1537 & 28° H8 / 3.Y. after the PP. [popes] abrogated"

70. *A Necessary Doctrine and erudition for any chrysten man, set furth by the kynges maiestye of Englande. &c.* (**Commonly known as** *The King's Book.*) **London: Thomas Berthelet, 1543.**

This is the "revised" *Bishops' Book* (1537, *Item 69)*, now reflecting Henry VIII's conservative theology and, essentially, a statement of Catholicism without the pope. Once again, the sacrament of the mass consists of "the very precious body and bloude of our lorde,"[54] and justification is through God's grace, requiring repentance and penance. Good Christians are directed to pray for the quick and the dead and, indeed, the entire Christian community; but "al such abuses as heretofore haue bene brought in, by supporters and mainteiners of the papacye of Rome, and their complicies, concerning this matter, be clerely put away, and that we therfore absteine frome the name of purgatory, and no more dispute or reason therof. Under colour of whiche, haue ben aduansed many fonde and great abuses, to make men beleue, that through the byshoppe of Romes pardons, soules myghte clerely be deliuered oute of it, and released out of the bondage of sin."[55]

The factotum block used on the title page bears the date 1534, the date of its first use. Publishers reused such borders, as convenient, with appropriate text inserted into the central compartment, but, apparently, with no great concern over any possible confusion over publication date. This block was used, with "1534" intact, until 1567.[56]

Both *The Bishops' Book* and *The King's Book* were printed in large numbers but they were heavily used and they are, today, quite rare.

---

54. Fol. F6[R].
55. Fol. U3[V]f.
56. R. B. McKerrow & F. S. Ferguson, *Title-page Borders used in England & Scotland 1485–1640* (London: 1932) p. 30.

The King's Book was published simultaneously on May 29, 1543 in several formats. In addition to this copy, STC records only two imperfect copies of this format in America.

71. *Certayne Sermons, or Homelies, appoynted by the kynges Maiestie, to be declared and redde . . . in . . . churches . . . .* **London: Rychard Grafton, 1548.**

The prescribed sermons of the Reformed Church of England, first published a year earlier, soon into the reign of Edward VI, and in use in revised forms for nearly a century. The twelve texts, composed by Cranmer, Latimer, Bonner, Becon, and Harpsfield, were imposed upon the clergy in place of "creative" preaching, which might be religio-politically incorrect in an England now Protestant. No omissions or additions were permitted, and even during the reign of Elizabeth independent Sunday sermons were restricted to the universities, the court, and St. Paul's Cathedral, save for special, specifically licensed events (funerals, weddings, city convocations, etc.). The content and even the phraseology of "the homilies" therefore remained as familiar to the English church-goer of the sixteenth century as anything but the liturgy itself. This volume is now rare; STC records only three other copies in America, one of which is imperfect.

The book is open to "An Homilie of the Salvacion," the sermon which sets out the reformist tenet of justification by faith alone. *(See illustration, facing page.)*

72. **Thomas [Cranmer], archbishop of Canterbury.** *A defence of the trve and catholike doctrine of the sacrament . . . .* **London: Reynold Wolfe, 1550.**

Thomas Cranmer was the architect of an English Protestantism which avoided the doctrinal and liturgical extremes of Roman Catholicism and continental Protestantism. Cranmer's "true and catholike doctrine" is, of course, English Protestant. This book is a denunciation of the Roman Catholic view of transubstantiation and is one of the basic texts of the reformed Church of England. *(See Item 66 for Cranmer's portrait.)*

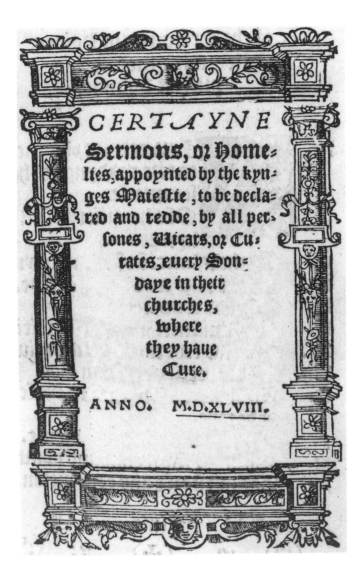

Item 71

Book of Homilies (title page) (1548)

73. Stephen [Gardiner], bishop of Winchester. *An explication and assertion of the true Catholique fayth . . . .* [Rouen: Robert Caly], **1551.**

Gardiner was a firm, traditional Catholic and this book was written in defense at his trial presided over by Protestant Archbishop Cranmer in 1550. Gardiner survived the Edwardian Protestant years and went on to become, along with Edmund Bonner, bishop of London, a chief persecutor of Protestants during the Marian reaction. Gardiner's book was published in Rouen, where it was safe to print Catholic doctrine during Edward's reign; it is ironic to note that in more conservative religious periods, during the reigns of Henry VIII and Mary I, it was Gardiner's religious enemies who were forced to seek publication abroad.

The book is open to Gardiner's discussion of the actual presence of Christ's body in the sacrament, one of the key points of controversy between traditional Roman Catholics and the more radical reformers.

74. *A Short Catechisme, or playne instruction, conteynynge the summe of Christian learninge, sett fourth by the kings maiesties authoritie . . . To thys Catechisme are adioyned the [42] Articles agreed vpon by the Bishoppes . . . .* London: Ihon [i.e. John] Day, **1553.**

The forty-two articles of religion were composed by Archbishop Thomas Cranmer after much debate and discussion; they were promulgated as the definitive statement of faith in Protestant England on 19 June 1553, and all clergy were instructed to conform to them. On 6 July, however, Edward died and he was succeeded by his half-sister, Mary, a devout Roman Catholic; that was the end of the forty-two articles. However, with rather substantial revision, they were reinstituted as the thirty-nine articles under Elizabeth I which are still the official doctrine of the Church of England.

At least partially due to Mary's accession so soon after this volume's publication, this book is now rare; STC records only two additional copies in America.

75. Nicholas Ridley and Hugh Latimer. *Certen godly . . . confer-ences / betwene . . . Nicolas Rydley . . . and Hughe Latymer . . . during the tyme of theyr emprysonmentes. Wherunto is added. A Treatise agaynst the errour of Transubstantiation made by . . . Nicolas Rydley.* [Strassburg: heirs of W. Rihel], 1556.

Ridley, former bishop of London, and Latimer, former bishop of Winchester, were the two principal Protestant martyrs burned as heretics in Oxford in 1555. They were fastened to the stake with a chain around their middles and the fire was lighted. "Be of good comfort, Mr. Ridley and play the man," said Latimer as the first burning faggot was laid at his feet, "we shall this day light such a candle by God's grace in England, as I trust shall never be put out."[57] See Foxe's *Book of Martyrs*, Item 77, for an illustration of these ghastly executions.

This book is a report of Ridley and Latimer's "conversations," which were really a "correspondence," while they were imprisoned and awaiting execution for their beliefs. The book was very popular and three editions were published in 1556, the year following their deaths.

Shown here is Ridley's "Treatise against the error of Transubstantiation" in which he makes the reformist argument that the host simply *represents* the body of Christ and is not, as the Roman Catholics held, miraculously transformed through priestly intervention into the *real* body of Christ.

76. [John Aylmer]. *An Harborovve for Faithfvll and Trevve Svbiectes, agaynst the late blowne Blaste, concerninge the Gouernment of VVemen . . . Anno. M.D.lix. . . . At Strasborowe the 26. of Aprill.* [i.e. London: John Day, 1559.]

This is the first edition, second issue (with added preface and errata), of the most important reply to John Knox's inflammatory *Faithful Admonition unto the Professors of God's Truth in England* and *First Blast of the Trumpet against the Monstrous Regiment of Women* (both Geneva, 1558), ill-timed books assailing Queen Mary, which deeply offended the new queen, Elizabeth I. Knox had attacked rule by a woman as being unnatural and against the laws of both God and nature, but his quarrel was equally with the rule of a *Catholic* woman.

---

57. John Foxe, *Actes and Monuments . . .* (London: 1684) III, p. 430.

Aylmer, a Marian exile, defended female monarchy, even in its religious authority, and exhorted Elizabeth's subjects to obey her and, in addition, not demand her marriage. Ultimately, Aylmer found England to be "paradise"; after all, he said, "God is English."[58] As a result of his writings, which called for the English and Scots to overthrow their female rulers by force, Knox was *persona non grata* in England until after Elizabeth's death in 1603; Aylmer returned to England to a series of preferments, culminating in the bishopric of London.

The false "Strasborowe" imprint is odd, given Elizabeth's accession five months prior, and coronation three months prior, to the book's publication. Perhaps Day was taking no chances, on either side of the politico-religious aisle, so soon after the Marian persecutions.

77. John Fox[e]. *Acts and Monuments of Matters Most Special and Memorable . . . in the Church.* (Commonly known as *Foxe's Book of Martyrs.*) London: The Company of Stationers, 1684. Three volumes.

First published in 1563, this book was an extremely popular item in Protestant households, second only to the Bible. Giving a history of the Church from its beginnings up to the time of the book's printing, it took a fiercely Protestant viewpoint and went through many editions and printings over the next two centuries. Written in Latin, and "translated into Tudor English, often verbose but sometimes vivid and arresting, [Foxe's] history seemed to contemporaries to possess an unimpeachable authority. They received it as gospel truth—an English supplement to the Acts of the Apostles."[59]

---

58. And in 1644, in *Areopagitica*, his famed speech for the liberty of unlicensed printing, John Milton wrote: ". . . the favour & the love of heav'n we have great argument to think in a peculiar manner propitious and propending towards us. Why else was this Nation chos'n before any other, that out of her as out of *Sion* should be proclaim'd and sounded forth the first tidings & trumpet of Reformation to all *Europ*. And had it not bin the obstinat perversnes of our Prelats against the divine and admirable spirit of *Wicklef*, to suppresse him as a schismatic and *innovator*, perhaps neither the *Bohemian Husse* and *Jerom*, no nor the name of *Luther*, or of *Calvin* had bin ever known: the glory of reforming all our neighbours had bin compleatly ours. . . . God is decreeing to begin some new and great period in his Church, ev'n to the reforming of Reformation it self: what does he then but reveal Himself to his servants, & as his manner is, first to his English-men . . ." (John Milton, *Areopagitica; A Speech of Mr. John Milton for the Liberty of Unlicenc'd Printing, to the Parlament of England* (Hammersmith: 1907) p. 59f.)

59. John Adair, *Puritans: Religion and Politics in Seventeenth-Century England and America* (Phoenix Mill [Gloucestershire]: 1998) p. 58.

Item 77

The burning of Ridley and Latimer from Foxe's *Book of Martyrs* (1684)

Shown here is the burning, for heresy, of Bishops Ridley and Latimer. Ridley's death was particularly gruesome: a poorly built fire
that burned slowly caused him to cry out "Let the fire come unto
me, I cannot burn, I cannot burn."

Also exhibited *(Item 75)* is a volume of Ridley and Latimer's "con-
ferences" preceding their executions. *(See illustration, page 73.)*

78. [Richard Day]. *A Booke of Christian Prayers, collected out of the
ancient writers, and best learned in our time, worthy to be read with
an earnest mind of all Christians, in these dangerous and troublesome daies, that God for Christes sake will yet still be mercifull vnto
vs.* (**Commonly known as** *Elizabeth's Prayer Book.*) **London:
Richard Yardley, and Peter Short, for the assignes of Richard
Day, 1590.**

This is the third edition of a book first published in 1578, modeled on John Day's 1569 *Christian Prayers and Meditations,* and
republished in 1581. "Richard and John Day collaborated in the
production of what are, in effect, Protestant books of hours that pay
tribute throughout to Elizabeth as Reformation Queen. In an out-
standing example of iconoclasm, Elizabeth receives the place of
honor in collections of prayers comparable to the *Horae,* in which
the Blessed Virgin Mary once reigned supreme as Mother of God
and Queen of Heaven."[60] *(Compare with Item 68, a 1534 Book of
Hours.)*

This volume is distinctly both Protestant and English. For example, one prayer says:

> Amongest vs Englishmen here in England, after so great stormes of
> persecution, and cruel murther of so many Martyrs, it hath pleased
> thy grace to geue vs these Alcyon daies, whiche yet we inioy, and be-
> seech thy mercifull goodnesse still they may continue.

> But here also (alacke) what shoulde we say; So manie enimies we
> haue, that enuie vs this rest and tranquilitie, and do what they can
> to disturbe it. They which be friendes and louers of the Byshop of
> Rome, although they eate the fat of the land, and haue the best
> preferments and offices, and liue most at ease and aile nothing: yet
> are they not there with content. They grudge they mutter and mur-
> mur, they conspire and take on against vs. It fretteth them that we

60. John N. King, *Tudor Royal Iconography: Literature and Art in an Age of Religious
Crisis* (Princeton: 1989) p. 114.

liue by them, or with them, and cannot abide that we should draw the bare breathing of the aire, when they haue all the most libertie of the land.

And albeit thy singular goodnesse hath giuen them a Queene so calme, so patient, so mercifull: more like a naturall mother then a Princesse, to gouerne ouer them, such as neither they nor their ancestors euer read of in the stories of this land before: yet all this will not calme them, their vnquiet spirite is not yet content: they repine and rebell and needes would haue with the frogges of Esope, a ciconia[61], an Italian straunger, the Bishop of Rome to play Rex ouer them, and care not if all the world were set a fire, so that they with their Italian Lord might raigne alone. . . . That is it which they woulde haue, and long since woulde haue had theyr wils vpon vs, had not thy gracious pitie and mercie raised vp to vs this our mercifull Queene of thy seruant Elizabeth, somewhat to stay their furie. For whome as we most condignly giue thee thankes: so likewise we beseech thy heauenly Maiestie, that as thou hast giuen her vnto vs, and hast from so manifold daungers preserued her before she was Queene: so now in her royall estate: she may continuallie be preserued not only from ye handes, but from all malignant deuises wrought, attempted, or conceiued of enemies both ghostly and bodily against her.[62]

Open to the initial portrait of Queen Elizabeth at prayer, which engendered the book's common name. Note the symbols of royal power near her feet: the sword, the scepter, and her coat of arms. Her gown, the draperies, and the wall hangings bear Tudor roses and the coat of arms includes *fleurs de lis*, symbolic of England's continuing pretensions in France.

79. [John Udall (?)]. *A Dialogve, concerning the strife of our Churche: Wherein are aunswered diuers of those vniust accusations, wherewith the godly preachers and professors of the Gospell, are falsly charged; with a briefe declaration of some such monstrous abuses, as our Byshops haue not bene ashamed to foster.* **London: Printed by Robert Walde-graue, 1584.**

"Under the mild rule of Edmund Grindal as archbishop of Canterbury from 1576 till his death in 1583 . . . the Puritan movement in

---

61. A stork, which was felt to share many characteristics with a vulture.
62. Fol. H3^{V}ff.

England made considerable progress. . . . When John Whitgift . . . succeeded Grindal . . . his first concern was to reinstate uniformity of liturgical observance. . . . All ministers were once again required to subscribe or suffer deprivation of their livings and benefices; and once again the Puritan ministers rose up in protest. . . . The year 1584 was an important one for Puritan publications. . . . Many works which later came to be regarded as fundamental to the movement were published by the zealous printer, Robert Waldegrave. [Among these was] *A Dialogue, concerning the strife of our Churche*, attributed [but not certainly] to John Udall, a minister at Kingston, the first of a series of such Puritan dialogues."[63]

The title page succinctly describes the book's contents; shown is a passage where Orthodoxos, a divine, replies to an accusation that the Puritans teach disobedience, saying "as for the Puritans, their doctrine and practize is this: That men must obey ye higher powers under paine of damnation: but when any thing is commanded which is against gods word, we must obey God rather then men."

80. Richard Bancroft. *A Sermon Preached at Paules Crosse the 9. of Februarie [1588/89] . . . Wherein some things are now added, which then were omitted, either through want of time, or default in memorie.* London: Imprinted by E[dward] B[ollifant] for Gregorie Seton, 1588 [i.e. 1589].

This volume is the first edition of a sermon which Patrick Collinson, an historian of the English Reformation, described as "rightly regarded as a minor landmark in English Church history" offering "a foretaste of [Bancroft's] forensic ruthlessness in polemic controversy."[64] In this famous and oft-republished public exercise, Bancroft, the future archbishop of Canterbury, attacked the proliferation of Puritan objections to Elizabethan Church discipline as troublesome, incendiary and "schismatic," and even to be lumped with papist doctrine as "heretical." To the "factious clergy," stigmatized as "false prophets" like their biblical and latter-day forebears (Arians, Donatists, Anabaptists, Brownists), he linked "the lay factions"—*i.e.* anyone who had supported the radicals, or encouraged them in England or Scotland. "Never had Paul's Cross heard such a confident defense of the established Anglican polity,"[65] remarked

63. Peter Milward, *Religious Controversies of the Elizabethan Age* (London: 1977) pp. 77-9.
64. Patrick Collinson, *The Elizabethan Puritan Movement* (Los Angeles: 1967) p. 397.
65. Ibid.

Collinson, and Bancroft's simplistic and restrictive prescriptions deserve repetition:

> Reade the scriptures, but with sobrietie. If any man presuming upon his knowledge, seeke farther than is meete for him: (besides that, he knoweth nothing as he ought to know), he shall cast himselfe into a labirinth and never finde that he seeketh for. . . . The doctrine of the church of England, is pure and holie: the government thereof, both in respect of hir majestie, and of our Bishops, is lawfull and godlie: the booke of common praier containeth nothing in it contrarie to the word of God. . . . Suffer not your selves, as it were bowles, to be easily turned hither and thither. . . . It is very unmeete you should hencefoorth be any more as children, wavering and caried about like little boates with everie winde of doctrine by the deceit of men, and with craftines, whereby (as men that are wel practised) they lie in wait to deceive: but follow the truth in love, and in all things grow up as true and lively members of that bodie whereof Christ is the head.[66]

Bancroft's words regarding "seeking farther than is meete" remind one of the objections that the Roman Church had with biblical text being translated into vernaculars; Bancroft is concerned with heretical poisoning of Church doctrine, although he cloaks it in words that might suggest the laity's frustration in understanding religious complexities.

One should also note the length of this document, some 106 pages of text; people stood for hours outside St. Paul's Cathedral to hear the words that would assist in their salvation.

This volume is now rare; STC records only two other copies in America.

---

66. Pp. 42, 89–90, 105–6, slightly repunctuated.

Item 82

"Henry VIII Monk Hunting" from A'Beckett's *Comic History of England* (1847)

VII

Humor

THE books exhibited in this section, while meant to make their readers smile, or even laugh aloud, were not intended only to be funny. There is an edge to the humor; authors and artists used entertainment as a vehicle for criticism of royalty and the upper class, and they made their points in ways where less jocular criticism might fail. The pseudonym used by the publisher of Item 84 said it all: "The Committee of the Society for Keeping Things in Their Places."

81. Thomas Rowlandson. *Miseries of Human Life.* **London: R. Ackermann, 1808 [1823–25].**

In this volume, the artist Thomas Rowlandson satirized the problems of the upper classes in coping with the difficulties of their daily existence. The text of the exhibited illustration, entitled "Miseries of Public Places," reads, "After the play, on a raw wet night, with a party of ladies, fretting and freezing in the outer lobbies, and at the street doors of the theatre, among chairmen, barrow-women, yelling link boys, and other human refuse, in endless attempts to find out your servant, or carriage, which when found out at last, cannot be drawn up nearer than a furlong from the door." How different is it now on a winter's night in London's West End or New York's Broadway?

82. Gilbert Abbott A'Beckett. *The Comic History of England.* **London: Punch Office, July 1846–February 1848. Twenty parts in nineteen wrappers.**

A'Beckett's pun-filled *Comic History* is accompanied by twenty delightful, hand-colored engravings after John Leech and numerous additional illustrations in the text. A reader of the book should not be surprised to discover that both of the collaborators were veterans of the humor magazine, *Punch.* The exhibited illustration, "Henry VIII Monk Hunting," shows the king in hot pursuit of a monk who is fleeing his monastery with all the valuables he can carry.

Although generally found bound in two volumes, this copy is in parts, as originally published. *(See illustration, facing page.)*

83. *The Political House that Jack Built.* **London: William Hone, 1819.**

This takeoff on the nursery rhyme, "The House that Jack Built," is bitterly sarcastic, stating that the government's tax policies and wasteful royal spending were ruining the country. It goes on, however, to say that the press, "in spite of new Acts and attempts to restrain it, . . . will *poison* the Vermin, that plunder the Wealth, that lay in the House that Jack built." The "Dandy of Sixty" was, of course, the future George IV, at the time regent for his father, who had gone "mad." George was fifty-seven—not sixty—at the time, but sixty is older and better fits the meter! The illustrations are by George Cruikshank.

The exhibited pages are unopened and unbound sheets for this small book.

84. **[George Augustus Sala].** *Great Exhibition "Wot Is To Be" . . . By Vates Secundus [i.e. George Augustus Sala].* **London: "The Committee of the Society for Keeping Things in Their Places" [i.e. Ackermann], 1850.**

Sala's cartoon drawings of the "Great Exhibition Wot Is To Be" suggest that the great procession to the Hall of All Nations would include the Band of the Royal Life Guards, conducted by Prince Albert, "the most eminent instrumentalist of the day, . . . accompanied by a body of Exhibitors who will blow their own trumpets and endeavour to play first fiddle in a surprising manner."

England's Royal Line of Succession

HOUSE OF NORMANDY
WILLIAM I (The Conqueror) (1066-87)

WILLIAM II (Rufus) (1087-1100)

HENRY I (1100-35)

Adela — STEPHEN OF BLOIS (1135-54)

Matilda

HOUSE OF ANJOU [PLANTAGENET]
HENRY II OF ANJOU (1154-89)

RICHARD I (1189-99)

JOHN (1199-1216)
HENRY III (1216-72)
EDWARD I (1272-1307)
EDWARD II (1307-27)
EDWARD III (1327-77)

Edmund, duke of York

Richard, earl of Cambridge

Edward, the Black Prince

RICHARD II (1377-99)

John of Gaunt, duke of Lancaster   m. (1) Blanche of Lancaster
m. (3) Catherine Swynford

HOUSE OF LANCASTER

HENRY IV (1399-1413)
HENRY V (1413-22)
HENRY VI (1422-61, 1470-71)

John Beaufort, earl of Somerset
John Beaufort, duke of Somerset
Margaret Beaufort m. Edmund Tudor

HOUSE OF YORK
Richard, duke of York

RICHARD III (1483-85)

EDWARD IV (1461-70, 1471-83)

EDWARD V (1483)

(The Princes of the Tower)
Richard (duke of York)

HOUSE OF TUDOR
HENRY VII m. Elizabeth of York (1485-1509)

Margaret m. James IV of Scotland

HENRY VIII (1509-47)

Mary

m. (1) **Catherine of Aragon**   (2)   m. (4) **Anne of Cleves**
m. (2) **Anne Boleyn**   m. (5) **Catherine Howard**
m. (3) **Jane Seymour**   m. (6) **Catherine Parr**

Arthur, Prince of Wales
m. **Catherine of Aragon** (1)

England's Royal Line of Succession

Frances

Lady Jane Grey

(3) EDWARD VI (1547-53)

(1) MARY I (1553-58)

(2) ELIZABETH I (1558-1603)

James V of Scotland

Mary, queen of Scots *m.* Henry Stuart, Lord Darnley

HOUSE OF STUART

JAMES I (James VI of Scotland) (1603-25)

Elizabeth

Sophia *m.* the elector of Hanover

CHARLES I (1625-49)

Mary *m.* William of Orange

JAMES II (1685-88)

MARY II (1689-94) *m.* WILLIAM III (1689-1702)

CHARLES II (1660-85)

ANNE (1702-14)

HOUSE OF HANOVER

GEORGE I (1714-27)

GEORGE II (1727-60)

Frederick, Prince of Wales

GEORGE III (1760-1820)

WILLIAM IV (1830-37)

GEORGE IV (1820-30)

Edward, duke of Kent

VICTORIA (1837-1901) *m.* Albert of Saxe-Coburg & Gotha

HOUSE OF SAXE-COBURG & GOTHA
[HOUSE OF WINDSOR FROM 1917]

EDWARD VII (1901-1910) *m.* Alexandra of Denmark

GEORGE V (1910-36)

EDWARD VIII (1936)

GEORGE VI (1936-52)

ELIZABETH II (1952-)

Charles, Prince of Wales *m.* Lady Diana Spencer

Items concerning names shown in bold face type may be located in the Index, page 85

{83}

INDEX OF EXHIBITED ITEMS

Numerical references are to item or footnote numbers, not to catalogue page numbers.

Authors, illustrators, and publishers are indicated in italic type. Titles, some of which have been shortened in this index, are indicated in bold type. Persons or places mentioned only in the introductory commentaries are not included in this Index.

INTRODUCTION

By Dr Megan Barford, Curator of Cartography
at Royal Museums Greenwich

*'Everything looks so fantastic, so utterly different from anything on the Earth,
even in the wildest and most desolate districts, that the astonished observer feels
himself in the presence of an alien world. The white mountains, the black shad-
ows, the tumbled expanses of shattered rocks, the huge craters, the profound
pits, the gaping cracks, the towering peaks, and the congealed lava plains are,
in every sense, unearthly and unreal.'*

Hugh Percy Wilkins, 1946[*]

When amateur astronomer Hugh Percy Wilkins (1896–1960) described the
experience of looking at the Moon through a telescope for the first time, he was
introducing readers to views which he himself spent a lifetime interpreting.
Learning to see, which for astronomers observing the Moon at this time also meant
learning to draw, took time and patience. It was through such laborious observation
that Wilkins resolved the dramatic landscape he described into the outline shapes
which characterise his lunar mapping. The map reproduced here is Wilkins's third
and largest lunar map, first published in 1946. Made with a 300-inch diameter, it
was reduced to 100 inches for publication.

Wilkins was born in Carmarthen in Wales 1896. His interest in astronomy
developed when he was a child, in a period when involvement in amateur astronomy
meant not just using, but also making, telescopes. The first of his telescopes were

---

[*] Hugh Percy Wilkins, *Mysteries of Space and Time* (London: Frederick Muller, 1955): 52